Will Schooling Ever Change?

This book is an insightful meta-narrative about schooling which explores the global natural experiment of the COVID-19 pandemic and its potential impact on school culture.

The proposed book discusses how the abrupt and somewhat forced digital transformation of schooling on a global scale (caused by the COVID-19 pandemic) did not change the educational status quo. It states that online teaching and learning failed to transform the role of the key school actors, students and teachers as well as the relationship between them, despite megatrends such as digitalisation, automation and the development of artificial intelligence. This focus text discusses why the global experience of distance education did not translate into a significant qualitative change and provides a theoretical framework which enables the reader to interpret and explain the processes that occurred during distance education, as well as understand why extraordinarily little (if nothing) has changed in school culture.

It will appeal to scholars and students from the sociology of education and from education studies, particularly those interested in school culture, innovation in education, online teaching and learning, curriculum studies and education policy.

Piotr Mikiewicz is a professor at the University of Lower Silesia in Poland. He is an author of numerous publications revolving around the concept of social capital and social effects of the educational expansion. He is also an expert at the Ministry of Education and Science in Poland as well as the Poland's representative in the OECD's International Education Surveys: PISA Governing Board, PIAAC Board of Participating Countries. Recent publications include *Social capital and education – An attempt to synthesize conceptualisation arising from various theoretical origins* (2021), *Educationalisation and its implications for* *contemporary society* (2020) and *Socjologia edukacji. Teorie, koncepcje, pojęcia* (Sociology of Education. Theories, concepts, definitions, 2016).

Marta Jurczak-Morris is a researcher and a PhD candidate at the University of Lower Silesia in Poland, at the Faculty of Applied Studies. Having worked as a teacher in highly diverse primary schools in London in the United Kingdom, she has developed her professional and academic interests around issues such as class, social justice, educational inequalities, discrimination as well as the phenomenon of distance learning. Recent publications include *Pedants vs Mondains – On the Ways in Which Young People Interact in the Schooling Process Through the Lens of Pierre Bourdieu's Theory of Habitus and Socio-Cultural Capital* (2021) and *The Emerging New School Culture with Its Potential Consequences in the Context of Distance Learning During the COVID-19 Pandemic?* (2021).

Routledge Advances in Sociology

Towards a Sociology of Selfies
The Filtered Face
Maria-Carolina Cambre and Christine Lavrence

Social Cohesion in European Societies
Conceptualizing and Assessing Togetherness
Bujar Aruqaj

Governing Families
Problematising Technologies in Social Welfare and Criminal Justice
Rosalind Edwards and Pamela Ugwudike

Class, Trauma, Identity
Psychosocial Encounters
Giorgos Bithymitris

Protest in Late Modern Societies
Dynamics, Forms, Futures
Edited by Monika Banaś and Ruslan Saduov

Virtually Lost
Young Americans in the Digital Technocracy
Garry Robson

Will Schooling Ever Change?
School Culture, Distance Learning and the COVID-19 Pandemic
Piotr Mikiewicz and Marta Jurczak-Morris

For more information about this series, please visit: https://www.routledge.com/Routledge-Advances-in-Sociology/book-series/SE0511

Will Schooling Ever Change?
School Culture, Distance Learning and the COVID-19 Pandemic

Piotr Mikiewicz
Marta Jurczak-Morris

LONDON AND NEW YORK

First published 2023
by Routledge
4 Park Square, Milton Park, Abingdon, Oxon OX14 4RN

and by Routledge
605 Third Avenue, New York, NY 10158

Routledge is an imprint of the Taylor & Francis Group, an informa business

© 2023 Piotr Mikiewicz and Marta Jurczak-Morris

The right of Piotr Mikiewicz and Marta Jurczak-Morris to be identified as authors of this work has been asserted in accordance with sections 77 and 78 of the Copyright, Designs and Patents Act 1988.

The Open Access version of this book, available at http://www.taylorfrancis.com, has been made available under a Creative Commons Attribution-Non Commercial-No Derivatives 4.0 license. The Open Access fee was funded by University of Lower Silesia and NAWA Intervention Grants: PPN/GIN/2020/1/00051.

This publication has been funded by the Polish Agency for the Academic Exchange (NAWA) under an Intervention Grant *"The emerging new school culture with its potential consequences in the context of distance learning during the COVID-19 pandemic."*

Trademark notice: Product or corporate names may be trademarks or registered trademarks, and are used only for identification and explanation without intent to infringe.

British Library Cataloguing-in-Publication Data
A catalogue record for this book is available from the British Library

Library of Congress Cataloging-in-Publication Data
Names: Mikiewicz, Piotr, author. | Jurczak-Morris, Marta, author.
Title: Will schooling ever change? : school culture, distance learning and the Covid-19 pandemic / Piotr Mikiewicz, Marta Jurczak-Morris.
Description: Abingdon, Oxon ; New York, NY : Routledge, 2023. | Series: Routledge advances in sociology | Includes bibliographical references and index.
Identifiers: LCCN 2022058303 (print) | LCCN 2022058304 (ebook) | ISBN 9781032428581 (hardback) | ISBN 9781032428659 (paperback) | ISBN 9781003364627 (ebook)
Subjects: LCSH: Educational change. | Social distancing (Public health) and education. | Educational sociology. | COVID-19 Pandemic, 2020- | Education and globalization.
Classification: LCC LB2806 .M438 2023 (print) | LCC LB2806 (ebook) | DDC 371.2--dc23/eng/20221228
LC record available at https://lccn.loc.gov/2022058303
LC ebook record available at https://lccn.loc.gov/2022058304

ISBN: 978-1-032-42858-1 (hbk)
ISBN: 978-1-032-42865-9 (pbk)
ISBN: 978-1-003-36462-7 (ebk)

DOI: 10.4324/9781003364627

Typeset in Times New Roman
by KnowledgeWorks Global Ltd.

Contents

List of Figures and Table ix

Introduction 1

1 Education during the time of the pandemic 4

Introduction 4
An overnight transformation of how COVID-19 changed schooling 5
Technical and organisational adjustments of educational settings at the time of the coronavirus outbreak in Poland and England 8
   Duration of school closures and pandemic measures in school 10
   Synchronous and asynchronous models of distance education 14
   Exams 15
Distance education during the global pandemic – Main issues and perspectives 16
   Teachers' perspective 16
   Pupils' perspective 17
   Leaders' perspective 18
   Parents' perspective 20
Issues 21
   Digital divide 21
   Assessment 24
   Childcare as the most crucial function of schooling 25
   Governments' response in the situation of (the COVID-19) crisis vs public expectation 26

viii Contents

    Paradoxes 27
    Conclusion 28

2 School in its essence   31

    Introduction 31
    Schooled society – The logic of schooling in
      modern society 32
      Origins of mass education 32
      Different forms, one logic 42
    Institutionalisation, socialisation and
      allocation – Mechanisms of schooling
      from sociological perspectives 44
      Schools as institutions 52
      Schools as spaces of socialisation 53
      Schools as a tool of allocation 54
    The comprehensive model of schooling – Synthesis 55
    Conclusion 70
    Notes 71

3 Potential direction of change looking forward   72

    Introduction 72
    What happened – An interpretation of the crisis 73
      How do you build a repertoire of teacher
      and student roles? 73
      How do you monitor compliance with the norm
      of pedagogical relationship and motivate the
      parties to perform their roles accordingly? 74
      What about socialisation? 77
    Potential changes – Questions about institutional
      arrangements 80
    Potential consequences for the social functions
      of the school – Socialisation and allocation 84
    Conclusion 87

Ending: What comes next?   89

    Bibliography   93
    Index   104

Figures and Table

Figures

2.1	The logic of structural conditions of schooling – a systemic perspective	56
2.2	The logic of structural conditions of schooling – a micro perspective	56
2.3	A comprehensive model of schooling – synthesis	57

Table

2.1	Typology of research problems and interpretive perspectives within the sociology of education	49

Introduction

The topic of digitisation in education and schooling appears to be particularly important in today's post-COVID climate, during which scholars have endeavoured to make sense of the natural experiment that took place on a global scale in various aspects of social life as a result of the Coronavirus outbreak. One of the most 'sensitive and powerful' (De Silva Vieira, Barbosa, 2020: 30) of those aspects has undoubtedly been education and its foremost institution – school. Almost overnight, the latter transformed into an environment whose culture turned into a digital one – an institution that underwent such a significant change in terms of its functioning on both an organisational and technological level – that it seems unquestionable that school (with its culture) will never be the same. However, has this been the case so far? Has school changed, or does it need to change as a result of the pandemic? On the one hand, some scholars argue we are facing a widening digital divide concerning educational equality and social justice caused by distance education (Reay, 2020), which significantly exacerbated educational inequalities based on social class affiliation. On the other hand, others stress that online education will develop further against "prejudiced barriers that have been sustaining themselves in recent decades" (De Silva Vieira, Barbosa, 2020: 30) as part of the big reset that humanity is experiencing in the post-COVID world (Castells, 2020).

There are several crucial questions that need to be answered with regard to the phenomenon of distance learning and school culture. Firstly, has distance education, with its main features such as decompression of time and space (Castells, 2000), proven to be an opportunity for both pupils and teachers to redefine their view of what school should look like, as well as their role in classrooms with no walls and classes with no timeframe? Secondly, has it been a chance to reimagine the definition of the school situation (Goffman, 1990),

DOI: 10.4324/9781003364627-1

which constitutes "the beliefs, views, attitudes and relationships, and the written and unwritten rules that shape every aspect of the school as an institution (...) and community" (Ward, Burke, 2004: 1), otherwise known as school culture? Finally, has it only been a "survival strategy" during the time of crisis, or has it been an opportunity to revolutionise education and schooling?

The purpose of this book is to present an analytical framework that enables the reader to interpret the phenomenon of global dissemination of distance education during the COVID-19 pandemic as a missed opportunity for a potential qualitative change in education due to culturally instilled (and reproduced) perceptions of the role of the teacher and the pupil, which – at the same time – provide the ontological security (Giddens, 1984) necessary to recreate the order and continuity of the social world, including the micro-world of the school. Furthermore, the aim is to investigate the impact of distance education on school culture. Finally, the question has been raised whether there are any long-lasting effects caused by the experience of distance learning in a virtual setting in a post-pandemic school.

Even though there has been substantial research conducted in relation to the digitisation of education and its impact on teacher-pupil interactions, school rituals and, consequently, school culture (Crawford et al., 2020; Da Silva Vieira, Barbosa, 2020; Peach et al., 2020; Sa, Serpa, 2020; Gonzalez-Nieto et al., 2021; Kim et al., 2021; OECD Report, 2021; Tarabini, 2021; Olugboji, 2022), relatively little has been investigated in theoretical terms, with the use of analytical tools deriving from social theory. For this exact reason, this short book has been written. We have constructed a theoretical framework which enables academics, researchers, educators and postgraduate students to identify the underlying processes and rules across education systems, which keep its foundations in check and make them incredibly resistant to change.

Chapter 1 draws briefly on the general impact of the COVID-19 pandemic worldwide, with education at the very centre of this phenomenon. It further presents the cases of the Polish and British education systems and their different means of adapting to the educational crisis caused by the Coronavirus outbreak. Moreover, it attempts to capture the perspectives of key educational stakeholders in both countries – followed by the issues that arose during the pandemic – in order to demonstrate that despite the often-contrasting legal regulations and educational solutions, the underlying logic of schooling remains universal, irrespective of the education system of a particular country. These two countries therefore serve as case studies to portray key dimensions of the processes, which affected schooling during the COVID-19 pandemic. Our aim is to demonstrate the similarities of issues and perspectives despite differences of the school organisation as well as educational arrangements and traditions in both countries. This chapter is a starting point for more theoretically oriented analyses in the subsequent chapters of the book.

Chapter 2 provides a theoretical insight into the immanent features of school education – school(ing), exploring the concept of "schooled society" by unravelling the origins of mass education. Furthermore, it discusses two fundamental functions of schooling in modern societies: training and allocation and socialisation in the framework of institutionalisation from various sociological perspectives. Finally, the comprehensive schooling model has been proposed to interpret and understand the logic of school education with its persistence in time and universal character.

In Chapter 3, the proposed analytical approach enables the reader to interpret the key challenges that the education system had to face when implementing the distance education model. In addition, it helps us to understand why – despite numerous postulates of change and hopes for the revolutionisation of schooling – distance education during COVID-19 did not result in a significant change in educational practice and the logic of school education. Finally, the theoretical framework invites the reader to consider the potential social changes to transform formal education principles and its institutional arrangements.

As a final point, the proposed analyses are theoretical preliminaries and an invitation to discuss the model of analysis of the functioning of school education and the mechanisms of change in school culture. We place ourselves neither in the position of critics nor apologists for the educational status quo. Also, it is not our goal to evaluate the education system's response to the COVID-19 disruption. We propose an analytical model which encourages discussion about the experience of this Coronavirus crisis with the rigour of scientific analysis. At the same time, it is an opportunity to rethink the fundamental principles of the functioning of mass education institutions in modern societies.

1 Education during the time of the pandemic

Introduction

The experience of the crisis caused by the COVID-19 pandemic varied worldwide due to the differences in the functioning of entire social systems, including the institution of schools. Although schooling is a common feature of modern societies, no two education systems are the same. Their functioning is always a reflection of socio-cultural conditions, history, economy and the dynamics of political change in each country. Schooling is, therefore, unique and universal at the same time. The purpose of this book is to reflect on the latter by presenting a model of analysis, allowing the reader to pinpoint the underlying logic of schooling – which remains the same across all modern societies. As previously mentioned, the experience of the COVID-19 crisis took place within specific social and educational systems; therefore, we decided to look at the dynamics of the experience of the coronavirus pandemic in two divergent education systems (i.e., the British and Polish ones). Reconstructing their responses to the crisis enables us to identify the implicit and universal logic of schooling in both education systems, which – in turn – provides the basis for further analyses undertaken in Chapters 2 and 3.

Before introducing this chapter to the reader, it is important to stress that this book is a theoretical insight into the immanent features of schooling, not a comparative study *per se*. The cases of Poland and the UK have been presented here to demonstrate that despite two varying education systems, the general logic of schooling remains the same, irrespective of the country in which these education systems function. Therefore, the comprehensive model of schooling proposed in latter parts of the book serves as an analytical tool for any education system worldwide.

In the first part of this chapter, we draw a general picture of the pandemic and its global impact on societies, showing the complexity and

DOI: 10.4324/9781003364627-2

scale of this natural experiment, as well as how it affected a variety of aspects of social life (with education at the centre of it all). Moreover, this chapter engages in the current academic debate about whether the experience of distance education during the COVID-19 pandemic could be a catalyst for educational change and a qualitative shift from in-person, classroom-based education towards technology-based distance education, which comes in various configurations.

In the second part of this chapter, we briefly highlight the main characteristics of the Polish and British education systems and society before providing a description of the technical and organisational adjustments of educational settings during the pandemic in both countries, including aspects such as pandemic measures in schools, duration of school closures, models of distance education and assessment and exams.

Finally, in the third part of Chapter 1, we endeavour to encapsulate the perspectives of the main educational stakeholders: principals, teachers, pupils and parents of distance education during the coronavirus outbreak in Poland and the UK. Tellingly, their experiences reveal several critical issues that occurred during the remote model of teaching and learning, as well as those existing ones – which the pandemic unveiled and often exacerbated, provoking academics to ask big questions about schooling once again.

An overnight transformation of how COVID-19 changed schooling

Plenty has been written and said about one of the most challenging times in history that humanity had to face as a result of the COVID-19 pandemic. As societies, we have been "plagued" by the virus SARS-CoV-2 on multiple levels: physical (the first 15 months of the pandemic were marked by a 16% increase in mortality in comparison to the previous, pre-pandemic year), mental (a significant deterioration of well-being and rising levels of anxiety and depression across the nations), social (a growing sense of social isolation and disconnection from society) (OECD, 2021), economic (the situation of the pandemic has caused a lot of uncertainty and financial difficulty for one in three people across 25 OECD countries, triggering an unprecedented global economic crisis) (Borio, 2020; OECD, 2021) and, finally, educational level – where all the other dimensions intersect. Education has not only been hit the fastest (Castells, 2020) but also the strongest. The numbers speak for themselves: almost 1.6 billion pupils and students experienced unprecedented educational disruption in more than 190 countries across all continents (UNICEF, 2020). Moreover, 94% of the student population suffered learning losses due to school closures, with a staggering 99% of students from countries of low- and lower middle income (United Nations, 2020). To summarise, the pandemic "has wiped out 20 years of education gains" (United Nations, 2021: 13). This status quo stems from the decision of the World Health Organisation, which – on 11 March 2020 – declared COVID-19 a pandemic (Crawford et al., 2020) and thus forced schools around the world to undergo a rapid digital transformation to adapt to the new reality of living with the virus.

At this exact point, the unprecedented situation of the switch of worlds from face-to-face co-located education to a virtual, distance education setting seemed – to many observers – to be a turning point, after which there is no return to school as we know it. Overnight, the predictable and routinised school world turned into a virtual reality free from space and time limits (Castells, 2000); however, not free from its limitations. It goes without saying that education during COVID-19 was going through a major crisis, defined by some scholars as "the crisis of meaning" (Tarabini, 2021: 9) in relation to educational equality and social justice during distance education, which significantly exacerbated educational inequalities based on social class affiliation. Conversely, some social scientists have been looking at the bright side of remote learning, claiming that online education will develop further against "prejudiced barriers that have been sustaining themselves in recent decades" (De Silva Vieira and Barbosa, 2020: 30) as part of the big reset that humanity is experiencing in the post-COVID world (Castells, 2020). Moreover, amongst those scholars, Zhao and Watterston argue that the pandemic has been a once-in-a-generation opportunity not to waste the crisis, but to reimagine education instead (Zhao, Watterston, 2021) and, consequently, fundamentally change its culture, which "dialogues with the great social changes (macro) and internalises them with changes in pedagogical practices and processes" (De Silva Vieira, Barbosa, 2020: 33). Other academics state with certainty that change *will* happen, we just need to wait and see how it will look like (Fullan, 2020: 25).

It is truly extraordinary that education based on a long-standing Herbartian tradition of schooling, with its main institution, school, had been transformed globally almost overnight into a completely different "being". Suddenly, school premises became replaced by pupils' homes, where school bells stopped ringing, playtime chatter quietened down and school uniforms were put back in the wardrobes. Instead, all the learning was taking place with no physical presence of other school actors in a unique yet isolated virtual reality far from the school as we know it. In a blink of an eye, classrooms had become spaces with no walls and timeframe, where routines and rituals faded, and hierarchy and power dynamics were flattened (Castells, 2000: 15–16). This very decompression of time and space, which unequivocally has been one the main distinctive features of distance education, could rightly be seen as a chance to reimagine the definition of the school situation (Goffman, 1990) as it drastically changes the regionalisation and routinisation of schooling (Giddens, 1984), in other words, the *where* and *when* of learning (Zhao, 2020). For those reasons, it truly was an opportunity for a profound change in how we think about education and schooling. Specifically, about the role of a teacher and a student – as well as the relationship between them, otherwise known as "the pedagogical relation" (Znaniecki, 2001) – is culturally instilled in our minds and, hence, taken for granted. Thanks to the natural experiment of COVID-19, they could have been potentially transformed.

Over the course of a few days, countries around the world introduced distance education to tackle the issues arising from the pandemic; however, it is important to bear in mind that there is not one form of online education as it comes in a variety of forms and configurations, amongst which the main distinctions are synchronous vs asynchronous learning and blended vs hybrid learning (Ferdig, Kennedy, 2014).

The simplest and least stimulating form of remote learning is considered the so-called synchronous mode, when all the students attend "live classes" (from home) on screen at the same time (Zhao, Watterston, 2021: 8). As Zhao and Watterston conclude, this mode of online learning results in "distress, disengagement, and much less personal interaction and learning than traditional face-to-face situations" (Zhao, 2021: 8, see Darby 2020; Dorn et al., 2020). Therefore, escaping regionalisation (the *where*) but not routinisation (the *when*) does not provide the stimulus required for a better quality education as this type of learning is essentially no different to (or less effective than) traditional classroom learning.

Another model, proposed by Zhao and Watterston, and widely discussed in literature, is a more balanced approach based on conducting classes in a synchronous and asynchronous mode, where students would have a chance to work individually or in small groups and take advantage of the asynchronous learning, which would enable them to work wherever and whenever is most suitable for them. Once their task is completed, they would present their learning outcomes to the rest of the class and the teacher online during a synchronous class, having an opportunity to receive live feedback and further instructions from the teacher. Therefore, students would have freedom from the *where* and the *when* for a part of their learning, enabling them to work creatively and take ownership of their independent tasks. In contrast, the sharing of their learning outcomes and feedback would be given to them during a synchronous class, in a virtual presence of a teacher and peers.

Finally, an ideal scenario, according to the above-mentioned scholars, would be a mixture of distance and face-to-face (F2F) learning (Zhao, Watterston, 2021) – otherwise known as blended learning – as it enables students to engage in inquiry-based individual projects done in students' own time. It also promotes collaboration with peers and exposure to teachers' feedback and instruction in a real-life, face-to-face mode of learning.

Currently, in the midst of 2022, we have entered the post-COVID era (however, with the winter approaching, the situation might rapidly change, and the world could find itself in the middle of another pandemic spike). Nevertheless, so far, we have not seen a shift in global or even national endeavours to implement any of the proposed models (including blended learning) on a more regular basis. This book is an attempt to answer the question of why this has been the case.

Technical and organisational adjustments of educational settings at the time of the coronavirus outbreak in Poland and England

The UK and Poland have been showcased in this book as examples proving that despite two very different education systems, the underlying rules of the functioning of schools and the general logic of schooling remain intact. We intend to demonstrate that even though the Polish and British education systems vary significantly and reacted differently to the situation of the pandemic on both technical and organisational levels, the processes underlying their functioning during COVID-19 in relation to school culture were the same. This book provides a meta-perspective, explaining the reason why – irrespective of the education system – very little (or nothing) has changed in the functioning of schools after the natural experiment of the pandemic based on the patterns of school culture.

Before discussing the different reactions of the British and Polish education systems to the pandemic, it is vital to briefly present them as they vary significantly on multiple levels, including their vertical and horizontal structure, as well as their main characteristics derived from different historical contexts.

Poland is considered a relatively homogenous country even though recently, due to the Russian aggression on Ukraine, there has been a significant influx of Ukrainian refugees, resulting in 140,000 Ukrainian pupils joining Polish schools in 2022 (Głos nauczycielski, 2022). However, the issue of minority pupils in the Polish education system is not as stark as in the UK. Neither is the discourse of social class division, which, after the transformation of 1989 – when Poland became a democracy, had been uprooted from the public and academic debate for at least two decades due to its associations with highly unpopular theory of Marxism in Poland at the time (Gdula, Sadura, 2012).

In Poland, pupils begin their compulsory education at a slightly later stage (when they reach the age of six). They complete secondary school between the age of 18 and 20 depending on the type of school they choose (Kolanowska, 2020: 16). Their journey is split into two stages – primary stage (7–15 years old) and secondary stage (15–18 years old in the case of general secondary schools, 15–19 years old in the case of technical secondary schools and 15–20 years old in the case of sectoral vocational school – stages one and two). University courses take three to four years at undergraduate level, whereas postgraduate courses require another one and a half to two years of study. Completion of doctoral cycles takes three to four years (Kolanowska, 2020: 16).

The British education system is elitist and highly stratified, defined by a strong divide between state and private (independent) schools. This, subsequently, enhances educational inequalities and social class division (Ball, 1993: 17), with BAME (Black, Asian, minority ethnic) pupils being at a higher risk of disadvantage and deprivation (Reay, 2020). Diane Reay captured the phenomenon of class and its impact on British society in one of her well-known books "Miseducation. Inequality, education and the working class" conclude that

> The way class works in education shifts and changes over time, but what does not change are the gross inequalities that are generated through its workings.
>
> (Reay, 2017: 8)

When it comes to private schooling, Britain is famous for its high-profile public secondary schools, founded during late 19th century tradition, which are fee based and, therefore, not available to all the public even though "they call themselves public in a British sense" (Renton, 2017). Paradoxically, it is not Oxbridge universities (which, in principle, are accessible to everyone who meets their attainment standards), but public secondary schools that predominantly embody social class affiliation of their members as they are available to only a few members of the "class driven, fractured" British society (Scambler, 2020) and, hence, constitute class distinction in Britain (Sadura, 2017).

In the UK, the compulsory period of schooling starts relatively early as it runs between the ages of 5–16, covering primary and secondary education. This process is split into four "Key Stages": Key Stage 1 (5–7 years old), Key Stage 2 (7–11 years old), Key Stage 3 (11–14 years old) and Key Stage 4 (14–16 years old), which ends with the GCSE exam. (https://www.brightworldguardianships.com/en/guardianship/british-education-system/). If students choose to continue their educational journey, when they are between the ages of 18 and 19 (Years 12 and 13), they will be undertaking their preparatory years in sixth-form or in a college to complete their A-levels and, if they wish, begin their studies at university level (an undergraduate degree takes three years to complete, whereas a postgraduate degree usually takes one intensive year). A PhD research degree in Britain can take between two and seven years.

Over the past few decades, the pedagogical theory adopted by the British education system has evolved from a teacher-centred approach towards a more pupil-oriented approach, where the transmission of knowledge has gradually been replaced by pupils' active participation in the learning process (Tzuo et al., 2021: 558). In Poland, this significant shift in educational practice has started to occur; however, the scale of innovative teaching methodology is nowhere near as substantial as it is in British schools. Conversely, the dominant pedagogy in Polish schools remains the so-called spoon-feeding approach (Dehler, Welsh, 2014), based on the traditional interpretation of teaching and learning, gravitating towards a teacher-led educational practice.

Duration of school closures and pandemic measures in school

The UK and Poland responded to the spread of the coronavirus by shutting down schools (including nurseries) at the same time – the UK made their first lockdown decision on 18 March 2020, and Poland did so on 19 March 2020. In effect, both countries implemented COVID-19 measures on 20 March 2020. However, the way in which school closures were organised differed as both education systems reacted to the pandemic in their own way.

The pandemic timeline in the UK extends from 20 March 2020 to 8 March 2021, marked by two school lockdowns. The first lasted from 20 March to 22 July 2020 (even though the educational milestones within UK's home nations during the pandemic have been relatively similar, we focus mostly on the situation in England) (Cambridge Assessment, 2020a, 2020b, 2020c, 2020d). On 1st June, nurseries and preschools were reopened, and Years 1 and 6 pupils were allowed to go back to a school setting; however, at the end of June, the decision about distance education for Years 1 and 6 pupils was reintroduced due to rising concerns about the spread of the virus. Importantly, during this time, children of key workers and vulnerable pupils received face-to-face provision in schools (Cambridge Assessment, 2020a). As this lockdown marked the end of the 2019/2020 academic year, all exams were cancelled (Cambridge Assessment 2020b, 2020c). In the meantime, on 14th October, a new three-tier system of Covid-19 restrictions started in England, which is the reason why, throughout the pandemic, there were school closures introduced locally (Cambridge Assessment, 2021).

Schools in England reopened in September in order to reduce the potential risk of spreading the virus, most of them introduced so-called bubble systems in which students and staff members were only allowed to mix in with the same year group (Department for Education, 2021). Despite this precautionary measure, large groups of students, or sometimes even whole cohorts, had to self-isolate and effectively ended up learning from home despite schools remaining open (Coleman, 2021: 4).

A couple of weeks later, on 31 October 2020, the second four-week lockdown was announced and came into force in England on 5 November 2020, lasting until 2 December 2020 (https://www.instituteforgovernment.org.uk/sites/default/files/timeline-lockdown-web.pdf); however, schools, being the government's main priority, remained open (learning during the pandemic, 2021, gov.uk). Following this lockdown, the tier system was reimplemented, and on 19th December, the additional fourth tier was introduced.

Finally, the second national closure of schools started on 5 January 2021 and ended on 8 March 2021, when Boris Johnson – the Prime Minister at the time – presented a document called "Roadmap out of the lockdown" to the public, listing all the necessary steps that Britain needed to take to get back on track once and for all (Manyukhina, Hamlyn, 2021: 2). During the final lockdown, critical workers' children and vulnerable pupils were still receiving face-to-face provision in schools, while the rest of the students spent most of their second-term learning online ("distance learning"). In mid-March, when pupils went back to schools to receive in-person education, localised school closures were still in place due to local outbreaks of the virus (Coleman, 2021: 5).

In Poland, COVID-19 restrictions in schools lasted much longer – from 20 March 2020 to 20 February 2022. The Polish pandemic timeline appears to be quite complicated due to the differences in the extent and the time of the introduction of lockdown restrictions, depending on the school stage that pupils were at. In the case of primary and secondary schools, as well as higher education institutions, the so-called first wave of the pandemic (resulting in the first lockdown) lasted from 20 March to 26 June 2020. The second pandemic wave hit on 17 October 2020 and was followed by new lockdown restrictions, introducing a sanitary regime with division into yellow and red zones. Schools within the yellow zone used hybrid learning at a secondary and higher education level, whereas schools within the red zone offered students in secondary schools and higher education institutions access to distance education exclusively. Less than a week later, however, the whole country was declared a red zone, meaning that all schools started distance learning again.

The second closure of schools lasted until 17 January 2021. From then on, KS1 and lower KS2 pupils were allowed to come back to face-to-face learning, whereas others continued to work remotely. In March 2021, schools in certain districts were allowed to introduce hybrid learning as they turned from a red to a yellow zone; however, from 22 March until 11 April 2021, all students across primary and secondary schools had to go back to distance learning until 30 May 2021, when it was decided that all pupils across all educational stages could return to face-to-face learning.

Finally, the third closure of schools in Poland began on 20 December 2021 and lasted until 20 February 2022 – apart from KS1 and lower KS2 (up to Year 3) pupils, who were allowed to take part in face-to-face learning from 9 January 2022 onwards.

In summary, there are a few significant differences in the way schools organised themselves in Poland and Britain. First of all, during school lockdowns in Poland, all pupils were expected to access distance education from home, with no exceptions for vulnerable students or key workers' children, who – in the UK – received face-to-face education in school during both lockdowns. It is also clear that the British government prioritised in-person education and aimed to bring pupils back to schools as soon as possible, which is the reason behind the introduction of the bubble system to minimise the rate of infections and enable children to participate in face-to-face classes.

It is noticeable that Polish pupils, compared to their British peers, spent a lot more time during the pandemic learning remotely. According to the OECD data base, in 2020, the differences of the number of days when schools at all levels were closed are significant, if not staggering. Primary schools in Poland were closed for 77 days compared to 34 days in the UK. Moreover, the difference is even more significant when it comes to secondary schools, which were shut in Poland for 110 days, compared to 44 days in Britain. Finally, the greatest contrast can be seen at the higher education level – Polish higher education institutions were closed for 179 days, which is over three times longer than the British ones, closed only for 59 days (OECD, The state of global education: 18 months into the pandemic). Poland turned out to be one of six OECD countries (amongst Austria, Canada, Lithuania, Germany and Mexico) which continued distance learning in higher education institutions until 20 May 2021 and further (OECD, 2021).

Surprisingly, OECD and PISA general statistics regarding the situation of distance education in Poland and the UK show that Poland, compared to the UK, is a country in which students are better equipped to access distance learning in terms of home space (95% of Polish students, compared to 88% of UK students, have a separate place to study) and access to a computer (99% vs 96%). The situation is parallel when it comes to students from families of low socio-economic status, where 94% of Polish pupils have a proper learning space at home, while only 84% of British pupils meet this criterion. In terms of access to a computer, both countries performed similarly, with 98% of Polish pupils vs 93% of British pupils of low socio-economic status having access to a technological device, enabling them to study remotely. However, it is vital to highlight that between 2009 and 2018, there was a significant increase in the provision of computers to schools in OECD countries, with the most significant rise in the average number of computers per 15-year-old in the UK. In terms of internet access, the difference between Poland and the UK turns out to be very slight, with 99% of disadvantaged pupils in Poland having access to the internet, compared to 98% of pupils in the UK.

However, when looking at slightly more specific issues and related statistics – such as the degree of digital adequacy of computers in schools, high-quality internet connections and access to appropriate computer software – UK school institutions, compared to Polish ones, are at a much higher level of sophistication both on average per pupil amongst pupils from affluent families, as well as those from disadvantaged backgrounds. Indeed, the data is as follows: in terms of digital adequacy of computers, the UK reported 69% of schools meeting this criterion, compared to 51% of schools in Poland. In terms of high-quality internet connections, UK schools have a significant advantage with 79%, compared to 60% of Polish schools. The differences in access to appropriate software are even more significant (80% in the UK, 55% in Poland), showing a clear contrast in the degree of technological advancement between the two countries.

In the opinion of principals participating in the OECD survey, UK schools also outperform Polish schools in terms of ICT staff responsible for digital equipment, which is present in 70% of UK schools but only in 31% of Polish schools. The situation is similar with the use of effective platforms supporting remote education; their use in the UK reaches an average of 70% of schools, while in Poland, not even half as much – 37%.

However, when it comes to preparing teachers in terms of their pedagogical and digital competencies by ensuring that they participate in digital training, offering them sufficient time to prepare online classes and encouraging them to use technological devices during lessons, Polish schools lead the way in this respect. According to OECD data, Poland was amongst the five OECD countries where teachers were particularly encouraged to take part in digital competencies training to ensure high-quality distance education in 2021, as well as 2022.

Synchronous and asynchronous models of distance education

Initially, the most common way of delivering online lessons in Polish schools during the COVID-19 pandemic was based on a simple asynchronous approach with the use of email, chat and other communication platforms such as Topclass, all of which enabled teachers to provide their students with their learning activities. Moreover, teachers supplied pupils with paper-based activities they had created or retrieved from textbooks. Finally, they used digital educational materials from educational websites such as epodręczniki.pl or, simply, asked students to access educational activities on *TVP* (Public Polish Television) (Sel, 2020).

During the second wave of the pandemic, in autumn 2020, there was a noticeable transition (from 30% of teachers in March 2020 to 90% in October 2020) towards teaching "live lessons" online – so-called synchronous distance learning – with the use of MS Teams and Zoom, followed by higher expectations towards pupils (Całek, 2021). Finally, during the third COVID wave, from December 2021 onwards, the mixture of both synchronous and asynchronous approaches was implemented in the form of mixed distance education, providing students with a more balanced provision by trying to recreate school routines in a virtual setting (Całek, 2021).

During the first stage of the pandemic, British schools were mainly using downloadable learning packs, links to learning materials posted

Education during the time of the pandemic 15

on school websites and learning platforms, as well as well-established digital learning applications and online materials. Later in the pandemic, webinar-based lessons were introduced, as well as synchronous teaching in the form of "live lessons". Needless to say, there was notable disproportionality between private and state schools in delivering synchronous classes. According to the "Shock to the system" report, in private school settings, synchronous teaching was up and running on a regular basis, whereas in most state schools, live lessons were sporadic due to a lack of access to technology and/or the internet connection of some students, as well as due to the limited financial resources of state schools, followed by concerns about security and privacy issues online (Cambridge Report, 2020). Overall, from looking at the data collected by the Cambridge team, it is evident that at primary level, the majority of schools adopted the asynchronous model of distance learning. In contrast, secondary schools focused more on the synchronous approach. With regard to private schools, they put more emphasis on collaboration, providing pupils with technology to help them support each other, and focused less (compared to state schools) on asynchronous learning (Cambridge Report, 2020: 37).

Exams

Poland and the UK took a completely different approach with regard to GCSE and A-level exams during the pandemic. In July 2020, the UK's GCSE and A-level exams were cancelled as part of the exceptional measures introduced for exam grading due to the coronavirus pandemic. In reality, this meant that pupils "received the higher of a centre assessment grade or calculated grade for GCSE, AS and A level" (GCSE, AS and A level: Autumn and November 2020 exam series, gov.uk). There were many concerns with regard to the algorithm and methodology used to generate the grades (Cambridge Report, 2020); however, the autumn series was introduced for those candidates who did not have a chance to receive their grades in summer and for those who were disappointed and wanted the opportunity to improve it (GCSE, AS and A-level: Autumn and November 2020 exam series, gov.uk).

The following year, in January 2021, the government announced the cancellation of GCSE, AS and A-level exams that were due to take place in the summer of 2021 as it would be unfair towards students whose education had been disrupted by the coronavirus pandemic. Instead, the government proposed that teachers would be responsible for students' assessment and would allocate grades to pupils based on their performance using Teacher Assessed Grades or TAGs (Research and analysis GCSE, AS and A-level summer report, 2021, gov.uk).

Polish students, in turn, were asked to take their GCSE and A-level exams throughout the whole pandemic. In June 2020, Polish pupils sat their exams at both GCSE levels – known in Poland as the "eighth-grade exam" and A-level. The latter was required only in a written form, whereas the oral A-level exams were cancelled due to pandemic restrictions (Ministerstwo Edukacji i Nauki, 2020). The GCSE exams were delayed from April to June 2020, allowing students extra time to revise. The whole process was organised strictly and followed sanitary measures. In the following years (2021 and 2022), students were asked to take their exams in a similar form, with the exemption from the oral A-level exams – which were cancelled due to the virus.

There were quite a few controversies and concerns in Poland, as well as in Britain, around the governments' guidelines and recommendations – including the end-of-year assessment during the COVID-19 pandemic, which resulted in a decrease of public trust towards the government and its decisions (Cambridge Report, 2020: 33) (Całek, 2021).

Distance education during the global pandemic – Main issues and perspectives

Teachers' perspective

Both Polish and British teachers struggled with digital fluency as well as a pedagogical skillset to teach online and integrate teaching with technology during the COVID-19 pandemic. In Poland, for example, 85.4% of teachers had no experience with digital technology in teaching before the pandemic (Buchner et al., 2020). Consequently, the lack of teachers' digital competencies had implications for the quality of provision and contributed to a more reactive rather than proactive response to the pandemic in schools – known in the UK as Remote Emergency Teaching (RET) (Cambridge Report, 2020), whereas, in Poland, as Remote Crisis Education (Romaniuk, Łukasiewicz-Wieleba, 2022). The pandemic has revealed the need for high-quality digital education and, subsequently, high-quality training for teachers (that they often lacked), including critical thinking in order to provide a more interactive and effective online environment for pupils (Cambridge Report, 2020: 18).

In Britain and Poland, teachers struggled with time-consuming preparation, working longer than usual; assessment and monitoring pupils' progress turned out to be challenging. Polish and British teachers complained about slower pace of teaching online and difficulty hitting their teaching targets. Another important factor turned out to be the pupils' unpreparedness for online learning due to the completely different nature of virtual classes requiring self-regulatory skills which they often had not yet developed. Teachers were reporting a lack of motivation and independence amongst pupils (Gustiani, 2020) apathy, boredom and loneliness (Cambridge Report, 2020: 16), all of which significantly impacted their performance during distance learning. In addition, one of the key determinants of pupils' poor performance turned out to be the symptoms of the previously mentioned "digital divide", such as a lack of equipment, poor internet connectivity, a lack of (or disruptive) [learning] space at home (Ptaszek et al., 2020; Reay, 2020).

Despite these challenges, which had put educational practitioners in a "sink or swim" situation (Cambridge Report, 2021: 4), teachers in both countries quickly adapted to the new reality and developed their digital potential by supporting each other in an informal way. As Richard Holme described it, teachers' solidarity and support for each other during the COVID-19 pandemic was an unprecedented phenomenon (Holmes, 2020). When it comes to teachers' preferences of how to teach, the vast majority of British and Polish teachers prefer face-to-face teaching in the classroom (Cambridge Report, 2020), followed by blended teaching (the combination of face-to-face as well as distance education). Only a very small fraction of teachers opted for distance education as their preferred method of delivering the curriculum (Całek, 2021), which indicates that, in general, teachers perceive the distance education model as emergency education during a crisis rather than a chance for a long-term educational revolution. In effect, most teachers – as well as educational leaders – think of schooling in post-COVID times simply as "business as usual", putting the experience of distance education far behind, and with a deep sigh of relief.

Pupils' perspective

Numerous reports and analyses about pupils' educational attainment during COVID-19 in Poland and in the UK indicate a decrease in students' progress across all educational phases compared to the pre-pandemic year. Furthermore, the widest learning gap was reported amongst pupils from lower socio-economic backgrounds compared to the rest (Department for Education 2021; GL Assessment, 2021; RS Assessment, 2021). Apart from the evidently lower attainment – underpinned significantly by the digital divide amongst Polish and British pupils – according to Polish and British surveys, there were two main reasons why pupils preferred face-to-face education compared to online education. First of all, they value education in a traditional school setting as it enables them to interact with their peers. Second, the physical presence of a teacher gives them an opportunity to ask questions and receive regular feedback from teachers (Plebańska et al., 2020: 15; Manyukhina, Hamlyn, 2021: 4). Furthermore, pupils missed their school routines and found it hard to organise themselves at home (Stunża, 2020).

With regard to the positives of distance learning, British pupils enjoyed the freedom of expression – particularly during online art classes – emphasising the unlimited time they had to create their work as opposed to the very regimented schedule in a traditional school setting (Manyukhina, Hamlyn, 2021: 4). Moreover, pupils from primary – as well as secondary schools – enjoyed working from home during distance education for logistical reasons (i.e., they did not have to wake up early in the morning to commute to school, and they felt more comfortable at home than in a classroom). Furthermore, they enjoyed the freedom and the time flexibility as they were able to decide when and what subject they wanted to learn at a particular moment in time. Finally, pupils felt less distracted at home and enjoyed the peace and quiet of working from home (here is where the digital divide, again, comes into play) (Sekścińska et al., 2020).

Researchers from Cambridge, who ran a very insightful survey on educational stakeholders' feeling of enjoyment from distance learning after the first wave of the pandemic in June/August 2020, found that the group that struggled the most during distance education were the youngest learners (from the "Early Years' provision") as well as pupils with special educational needs. The second group which found it hard to muddle their way through the pandemic were educational leaders, followed by secondary pupils and teachers, respectively. Interestingly, the stakeholders who found distance learning the least challenging of all school actors were pupils' parents – yet still over 62% of them considered distance learning challenging (Cambridge Report, 2020: 8). In the British context, it is important to state that private schools had a much higher percentage of stakeholders' satisfaction from distance learning and, analogically, a lower percentage of dissatisfaction, compared to state schools (Cambridge Report, 2020: 8).

Leaders' perspective

In the UK, the educational leaders found the, often confusing, messages they were receiving from the British government with regard to the pandemic restrictions, with very little notice, incredibly frustrating. The ever-changing stream of policy advice (Cambridge Report, 2020: 33) was often unclear as to what was just advice or guidance, and what was a statutory instruction that schools were obliged to follow. Government guidance became "an uncharted and rapidly shifting territory" (Beauchamp et al., 2021: 1), changing at times overnight, or even mysteriously disappearing from the Ministry of Education's website (Cambridge Report, 2020: 33). In general, headteachers felt unsupported and confused and forced to make decisions based on incomplete information they were receiving from the government (Cambridge Report, 2020: 34). Therefore, rather than simply following the guidance, British headteachers had to first interpret, translate and, finally, implement it in their schools (Fotheringham et al., 2020: 1), which they found stressful and anxiety-breeding. On the one hand, educational leaders wanted to fulfil their duties to the best of their abilities with competence. On the other hand, they felt helpless and frustrated because they could not do so due to the government's chaotic performance on a communication and organisation level.

In Poland, the situation was similar – there was a lot of criticism towards the Polish government with regard to the way the pandemic was tackled. Polish educational leaders, similarly to the British headteachers, experienced a lot of uncertainty and confusion because of the disinformation they were facing during the COVID-19 pandemic. They were quite vocal about the fact that they needed clarity from the Polish government, as well as from the Sanitary and Epidemiological Station (known as Sanepid). The latter, together with headteachers, had the power to decide whether to close or to reopen a school, when the division of yellow and red zones had been introduced nationwide (Igielska, 2020).

Headteachers reported that at the time of the pandemic, when schools adopted the distance education model, they did not find chief education officers' advice or teacher training institutions particularly helpful since either the support they offered was not particularly relevant to schools' needs, or the leaders did not see any benefits from asking for their help (Sekścińska et al., 2020: 227). In summary, the national headteachers' survey confirmed a limited response from external institutions supporting schools such as school inspectorates, as well as pedagogical and psychological support organisations in the face of an abrupt, yet important, educational change such as distance education during the COVID-19 pandemic. In Polish leaders' opinion, educational institutions in Poland found it challenging to react quickly and effectively in the crisis that the COVID-19 pandemic had proven to be (Sekścińska et al., 2020: 227).

Parents' perspective

Parents' greatest worry regarding distance education during the coronavirus pandemic was the risk of their children falling behind in their learning, defined otherwise as the so-called learning loss. Overall, 56% of British parents taking part in the COVID-19 Parent Ping survey confirmed that the latter was their most burning concern (Cambridge Report, 2020: 23). Their answers stemmed from their perception of distance learning being ineffective and that certain subjects that their children were particularly interested in could not be taught online. Therefore, parents who were financially stable and able to afford extra expenses for their children's education during COVID-19 were spending money on additional resources such as books, subscriptions, accessing online educational apps and websites, as well as electronic devices. As Cullinane and Montacute report, most British parents spent less than £50 to support their children's distance learning in the first week [of lockdown], whereas 14% of parents spent more than £100 for this purpose – which demonstrates clear digital divides between families (Cullinane, Montacute, 2020: 1). In addition, 44% of pupils in middle-class families spent four hours (daily) learning from home. This was the case only for 33% of students from working-class families. When it comes to the parents' level of educational attainment, correlated with social status, children whose parents had an undergraduate or postgraduate degree were much more likely to spend more time learning per day due to their parents' cultural capital, providing them with confidence and comfort (Cullinane, Montacute, 2020: 5).

Despite all of these challenging factors, parents in Britain were generally satisfied with distance learning, with middle-class parents being slightly more positive compared to working-class parents (66% vs 56%, respectively). Analogically, parents of a higher economic status, whose children attended private schools, were likely to be satisfied with distance education than parents of children from state schools (Cullinane, Montacute, 2020: 1).

In Poland, parental perception of distance education evolved over time. Initially, as Całek indicates, Polish parents treated distance education like a survival test that they needed to "wait out". During this time, the responsibility for their children's learning had been almost entirely shifted from school (which, at the very start of the pandemic, did not have the tools to provide quality distance education) to children's homes, where they became teachers (Całek, 2021). In June 2020, Polish parents adopted a new strategy of waiting for the end of the school year and hoping that from September onwards, things will be

Education during the time of the pandemic 21

"back to normal". This period was marked by difficulties with pupils' assessment due to parents being often overly helpful, to the extent that teachers were not sure whose work they were marking – pupils' or parents' (Całek, 2021).

From September to December 2020, parents were under more pressure due to the fact that teachers tended to focus on pushing the pupils as much as they could, performing the so-called testosis (neologism from psychosis) by testing them more often than at the beginning of the pandemic, and regularly using "live sessions" based on the synchronous model of teaching (Całek, 2021: 4). This period was marked by a significant deterioration in mental health amongst pupils and their parents because of the online overload.

From January 2021, the dynamics had changed, and teachers tried to take a bit more of a balanced approach towards distance learning by introducing a "new normality", which was based on traditional school routines, including following the same timetable as a "traditional" school in a virtual setting and, thus, normalising the pandemic reality by transferring a pre-pandemic school to the online world. In June 2021, Grzegorz Całek created a survey and asked parents to summarise their experience of distance education in Poland. The three most common answers were failure, misunderstanding and mistake (Całek, 2021: 7).

Issues

Digital divide

The digital divide, which manifested itself with double force during the COVID-19 pandemic, further widened gaps between the rich and the poor in British schools and British society. Not only does it exist on a micro-level between individuals in society, but it also reaches the structural level by dividing families as well as schools – which makes it a systemic issue. It has a triple dimension which exists in hardware, software and technological skills (Reay 2020: 316) on the macro-level of schools and the micro-level of families. The digital divide equation involves three types of schools: independent schools, affluent state schools and state schools from the most disadvantaged areas (usually with the highest rates of the "free school meal" pupils). The differences between them in terms of the access to facilities such as online platforms to receive pupils work are striking – 60% of private schools had such access, followed by 37% of affluent state schools, whereas only 23% of state schools from the most deprived areas utilised online platforms to facilitate distance learning (Montacute, 2020: 1). Reports by SchoolDash and RSAssessment demonstrated that the youngest pupils from the most deprived areas suffered the most significant learning loss during the pandemic. Moreover, Pensiero and other researchers estimated that these pupils' learning attainment dropped by 31% across all the subjects from March to September 2020 at primary level and 28% at secondary level. In comparison, children from the most affluent areas lost 24% and 14% of their average attainment levels, respectively (Pensiero et al., 2020). Apropos secondary schools, the educational loss in reading at the beginning of autumn 2020 was 1.8 months amongst all the pupils; however, regarding the poorest students, it increased to 2.2 months. The data is even more staggering when it comes to primary school pupils, whose learning losses were estimated at 1.7 months for reading and 3.7 months for mathematics. In contrast, amongst the most disadvantaged pupils, they turned out to be even greater, rising to 2.2 months and 4.5 months, respectively (Education Policy Institute, 2021).

Research about the impact of COVID-19 on the functioning of English state schools, conducted by the Nuffield Foundation and National Foundation for Educational Research (NFER), concludes that the digital divide in England is a systemic rather than an individual issue (see Lucas et al., 2020; Sharp et al., 2020). It turns out that disadvantaged pupils who attend more affluent schools engaged in distance education much more than pupils of the same background in schools of higher deprivation. In other words, the level of school deprivation has a more significant impact on pupils' engagement in distance education than their low socio-economic family background.

In Poland, the phenomenon of the digital divide is equally overwhelming, even though the division between private and state schooling is nowhere near as significant as it is in the UK. The most apparent digital inequalities lay not in the access to electronic devices, but in the access to fast broadband, in the quality of the equipment as well as the cultural capital of pupils' parents – who, almost overnight, became their prime teachers during the pandemic (Długosz, 2022). According to a CenEA report, approximately 1.6 million pupils struggled to access distance learning due to those reasons. The data shows that 7.1% of students had issues with the internet connection, 17.3% lacked an appropriate, good-quality electronic device to take part in online classes due to having siblings with whom they needed to share the equipment. In addition, for 833,000 pupils, the lack of learning space at home was another challenge they had to face, which significantly impacted their educational performance during the pandemic

(Myck et al., 2020). It is important to stress that during school shutdowns in Poland, there was no in-person provision for the key workers' children and vulnerable students as it took place in the UK. All Polish pupils had to stay at home, with no alternative other than distance education. This ultimately contributed to the growing attainment gap between pupils of high socio-economic status and those from low income, mostly working-class families. As the Batory Foundation reports, during school lockdowns in Poland, one of the common practices amongst affluent families was hiring a tutor to support their children's education during distance learning, as well as spending time with their children and tackling online learning together. This was thanks to the flexibility they had due to their relatively high occupational status compared to most parents who had to go to work physically as they occupied lower ranked professions which, in most cases, did not require higher education qualifications (Frey, 2020).

Another concerning "side effect" of school shutdowns in Poland and Britain, which appears to be an aftermath of the digital divide, is the phenomenon of "disappearing pupils" (Ślusarczyk, Świątkiewicz-Mośny, 2020: 33) who simply vanished from teachers' sight during the pandemic and, in some cases, did not go back to school when lockdown restrictions were lifted. According to OFSTED reports, in October 2020, out of 121 inspections, a third of schools declared an increase in pupils' unauthorised absence or change to home-schooling (Shock to the system, 2021). A Teacher Tapp survey revealed that most middle-class pupils returned to school after the first lockdown, whilst less than a third of their peers returned to schools in more disadvantaged communities (Teacher Tapp, 2020). As Diane Reay noticed, this occurrence – even though unsurprising – is clearly against the neoliberal discourse, in which school is placed on a pedestal for being an ultimate rescue and a sanctuary for the poor and is a place where they can find shelter and protection. In reality, pupils from low socio-economic backgrounds feel that they do not belong there, finding education "an uncomfortable space of judgement and labelling" (Reay, 2020: 314), which explains the increase in their absence during the coronavirus pandemic.

When it comes to online lessons, the disparities are even greater. According to Teacher Tapp, at primary level, 60% of private schools had virtual classes as opposed to 11% of state schools – which were able to provide their pupils with such classes. It gets even worse when we look at secondary schools. Overall, 85% of private schools ran online classes compared to only 5% of state schools. Without a doubt, this shocking 17-fold ratio unmasks the scale of the issue of the digital divide in British education system during COVID-19 (Teacher Tapp 2020). The situation in which the poorest suffer the most is due to such basic needs as internet connection. This is often available to them only via a phone screen and is often slow and limited as their homes are "overcrowded and underequipped" and they experience "high stress and little solace" (Reay, 2020).

Assessment

The COVID-19 pandemic revealed struggles of education systems around the globe with pupils' assessment during distance teaching and learning, which resulted in a general rise in anxiety levels amongst all educational stakeholders: teachers, pupils and their parents.

One of the most problematic aspects of marking pupils' work turned out to be the element of (dis)trust, which made teachers question students about whether they had completed their work independently as, quite often, assignments and homework were delivered at a standard that educators had not seen before [from certain pupils]. A second challenging factor that comes into play is the element of low verifiability of knowledge and skills due to the limited student-teacher interaction in an online setting. The reason behind this status quo is that the current assessment scheme is inclined towards testing and remains oblivious towards the possibilities that effective online learning based on interaction and engagement brings to the educational table (Luckin, 2017).

Moreover, the coronavirus outbreak accentuated the importance of pupils' assessment as teachers' strategies for behaviour management, proving that grades also served other purposes, including maintaining discipline in the classroom and ensuring that students behaved appropriately. In the pandemic, both Polish and British teachers reported they felt helpless, as if they lost their "secret weapon" – assessment and grading, which they could use to control students and enforce expected behaviours (Mikiewicz et al., 2022).

In addition, teachers found the process of online marking incredibly time-consuming because of the decompression of time (Castells, 2000). This meant that, in the asynchronous model of teaching, they were receiving pupils' work at different times of the day (including late evening hours), which meant that their work-life balance was constantly disrupted. This, in turn, resulted in rising levels of stress and anxiety amongst teachers due to work overload (Cambridge Report, 2020; Sterna, 2020).

Parents were most worried about the children's potential learning losses (including their impact on the end-of-year assessment) and the pupils' well-being. The last two, like a causal pendulum, were highly interlinked. The main concern revolved around the effectiveness and fairness of the assessment methodology implemented by British schools to grade pupils' performance during distance learning.

Childcare as the most crucial function of schooling

Surprisingly, the situation of the pandemic emphasised one of the most basic yet latent functions of school, which most of the school actors, parents in particular, were previously taking for granted – childcare. The coronavirus crisis revealed the importance of the fact that children, for most of their time during the day, are looked after by the institution of school. It provides them with a safe environment where they spend at least six hours each day during the week whilst their parents go to work (or work remotely from home). During the school shutdowns caused by the spread of the virus, it had become clear how crucial this basic function of schooling was. It enabled parents to leave their children in a safe place where, first of all – and most importantly – they were taken care of and, second of all, they were educated and acquiring knowledge and skills that enables them to enter a suitable profession in the future as young adults. Furthermore, "depositing" children to school turned out to be crucial for key workers such as NHS employees or service and transport sectors' employees, who simply would not be able to do their job had it not been for the childcaring function of school available to their kids during the pandemic (at least in some countries, including the UK). Israeli Kibbutz communities are a clear example of the importance of the childcaring function of school, which plays a central role in reproducing social order on a micro- and macro-level. Their children live in the so-called children's houses along with their peers, seeing their parents only for a few hours each day whilst their carers go to work and provide for them (Rayman, 2014). This internal community organisation emphasises the importance of place – the "children's house" (commonly known as a school) – for the reproduction of the social order to sustain coherence within this community. When we look at schooling from a wider, global perspective, this is precisely the case. First and foremost, we need schools so that our children have somewhere safe to go while we, adults, go to work (or work from home). The educational function of schooling, even though crucial as a principle, comes second, as it gives way to its childcaring function due to its practical implications. Therefore, it would not be an overstatement to claim that the prime and most crucial function of schooling is childcare, not education itself.

Governments' response in the situation of (the COVID-19) crisis vs public expectation

Throughout the pandemic, there were visible clashes between individual parents' concerns and the governments' inability to address them. Constant tension between society and the government demonstrated the public's need for a strong presence of the state system, which was expected to make decisions and deal with the situation of crisis even though this very government – in a non-crisis situation – is often expected not to interfere, but to leave its citizens "to it" in the name of such democratic values as freedom and independence.

In this context, the COVID-19 pandemic turned out to be a social experiment during which the public trust in governments' (TIGs) decisions and experts' advice gradually eroded amongst nations from all over the globe. Research analyses (conducted by Gozgor) on the level of TIG across various countries during the coronavirus outbreak led to a general conclusion that there is a negative correlation between people's trust in the government and the government's decisions about educational arrangements during the time of crisis. This negative correlation was analysed with two measures of trust as dependent variables, such as Truthfulness of Government Communication (TGC) and TIG, which were the main indicators of trust (Gozgor, 2022: 564). In summary, the research has shown that the higher the level of individuals' education (and effectively, their income), the lower the level of trust in the government; however, the tendency of distrust towards the government during the pandemic was of a more general nature amongst individuals across countries worldwide.

The key reasons behind it were the lack of clear communication to the public, limited transparency in decision-making, as well as weak (or non-existent) preparedness of critical sectors (such as education) to function during the pandemic (OECD, 2022: 3). The level of mis- and disinformation from the government in both the UK and Poland, with regard to pandemic restrictions and general guidance of how to navigate the situation of crisis, let Polish and British society (amongst many others) down.

The OECD recommendations for governments and governing bodies worldwide are to implement effective crisis management, with an adequate response to the crisis and the preparedness for the recovery period. In order to foster public trust, communication with the public has to be based on targeted messaging of concrete groups clearly and coherently (OECD, 2022).

Despite this guidance, the question of whether or not governments around the world will ever be fully prepared to manage future crises still stands.

Paradoxes

Interestingly, there are certain paradoxes involved in discussing the phenomenon of distance learning; first of them concerns the EdTech industry in the UK. According to one of the Cambridge reports about the impact of COVID-19 on schools in Britain (Cambridge Report, 2020), London is considered to be the largest centre of EdTech industry in Europe. In this context, one would imagine that British capital would become a European hub of distance education's excellence, wide spreading the advanced use of technology across the British schools at the time of the pandemic. However, in reality, the latter were far from being technologically advanced or even digitally ready to take on a challenge of distance learning (Ferguson, Savage, 2020) – how could this be? The answer to this question provides to some extent another paradox, namely, the isolation of British education system from the technological advancement.

Despite distance education's long tradition, dating back to 18th century, which from 1994 became more popular in the UK, due to the successful performance of the Open University (the largest English university offering distance learning), remote education had not been integrated into the bloodstream of the British education system because of the latter's "siloed structure" (Cambridge Report, 2020: 18). Furthermore, the isolation of the British education system from the technological advancement manifested itself not only at the very beginning of the pandemic, during the first school closure beginning on 20 March 2020, but it also lasted till December 2020, over eight months into the pandemic, when most of the state British schools were still implementing the so-called RET (Cambridge Report, 2020). This approach involved copying and transferring teaching practices from the traditional school setting to the online setting, without adequate pedagogical methodology and tools, which would enable pupils to effectively engage with their learning (Cambridge Report, 2020). These *ad hoc* solutions were underpinned by the lack of digital infrastructure and delivery models, which indicates that Britain (just like the rest of the world) was not ready to successfully implement distance education half way through the COVID-19 pandemic.

Another paradox worth discussing in the context of the potential educational change during the coronavirus outbreak is the contradictive rhetoric around it, portraying distance education as a chance and a crisis simultaneously. On the one hand, the Head of the Education Division at the Organisation for Economic Cooperation and Development (OECD), Andreas Schleicher, talks about "a great moment" (Anderson, 2020), during which:

> All the red tape that keeps things away is gone and people are looking for solutions that in the past they did not want to see. Students will take ownership over their learning, understanding more about how they learn, what they like and what support they need.
>
> (Anderson, 2020)

On the other hand, the narrative about the pandemic and its impact on education systems around the world was saturated with derogatory terms such as educational emergency, educational crisis, disrupted learning and educational disruption (OECD, 2020a, 2020b, 2020c, 2021). Even though Andreas Schleicher attempted to address these mixed messages, which – one could argue – sound rather oxymoronic by claiming that "real change takes place in deep crisis" and that "you will not stop the momentum that will build" (Anderson, 2020). However, in hindsight, the momentum had passed as we are currently entering the post-COVID era and the real change in our education systems has not happened.

Conclusion

The issues and experiences of educational stakeholders during the COVID-19 pandemic presented in this chapter provide the answer to the key question of why little (if nothing) has changed in school culture. The accounts of teachers, leaders, pupils and parents indicate that distance learning during school shutdowns was a temporary solution that enabled them to survive the situation of crisis, not an alternative that opened their minds to different, innovative, potentially better ways of teaching and learning, what has been implied by Zhao and Watterston (2021: 9). The educational experiment of enforced distance learning was treated from the very start as an emergency rather than a chance to think and reimagine education. On 25 March 2020, Audrey Azoulay, UNESCO Director General, stated in her call for the creation of the Global Coalition for Education: "Never before have we witnessed educational disruption at this scale. Partnership is the only way forward. [Let's] draw the lessons of this crisis for the future of education" (UNESCO, 2020). It is striking that even though digital technology has been gradually introduced in schools over the past three decades, due to its rapid growth in advancement, particularly in the last ten years, schools found themselves unprepared digitally on both a methodological and technical level to smoothly navigate distance education on a long-term basis [during the coronavirus outbreak]. Instead, they plodded along, taking one day at a time and desperately waiting for the online learning "nightmare" to end. The most concise summary of what happened with schooling during COVID-19 is provided by a statement from the Cambridge Report:

> Nothing had prepared education systems to entirely reconsider a mostly universal education model based on attending school where learners and teachers work together in a classroom, with a weekly schedule carefully structured within an academic year, with high-stake exams taken by all at the same time, to be replaced in just a few months by entirely new models of education with digital technologies at the centre of it all.
>
> (Cambridge Report, 2021: 3)

This very reconsideration of our universal, in-classroom education model into a new one – with digital technologies being a crucial, not supplementary part of teaching and learning – would mean a school culture transformation. However, since education systems around the globe were not prepared to do so, school culture – at its core – remains intact. The reasons behind this status quo have, so far, been implicitly discussed in our narrative by referring to three key elements of the education system. First, we have looked at the bureaucratic and administrative reactions of Polish and British education systems to the pandemic, which represent the institutional aspect of schooling. Second, we have examined various organisational adjustments of the education systems, such as the assessment and exam regimes, which signify the selective and allocative function of schooling. Finally, we demonstrated technical changes within education systems where in-person education in a highly routinised school environment was replaced by distance education in a home environment, free from timetables, systems and rituals. This change during distance learning unfolded the third aspect of schooling – socialisation. In other words, distance education during the COVID-19 pandemic was nothing else but a reflection of traditional ("normal") school – a bureaucratic institution, subjected to the logic of assessment and grading, which apportions pupils on their career paths according to their educational attainment. School actors, teachers and students were still parts of the pedagogical relationship (Znaniecki, 2001) and played a ritual game imposed by the hidden curriculum of school (Jackson, 1968).

Therefore, socialisation, allocation and institutionalisation are the foundation of the education system as we know it and, at the same time, underpin the concept of schooled society discussed in the next chapter of the book, which offers in-depth theoretical analyses and explanations of these key aspects of schooling, referring to theoretical concepts of the sociology of education.

2 School in its essence

Introduction

The purpose of this chapter is to analyse the education system through the prism of school arrangements and their sustainability in the face of a significant impulse of (potential) social change (such as the experience of the COVID-19 pandemic). Before reflecting on specific processes involved in the education system's resistance to change, we need to understand the core logic of how the system works. In this chapter, we will attempt such a reconstruction by recalling how education and school(ing) are integrated into the logic of the functioning of modern societies.

In the first part of the chapter, we recall the origins of mass schooling as a response to the systemic demands of modernity. Subsequent analysis must see the interrelation of the logic of schooling with the nature of the new social order which emerged in the 18th and 19th century. The development of the mass education system is associated with modernisation, industrialisation and the origins of the nation-state, as well as with the development of the idea of individualistic subjectivity. The basic logic of the modern state and economy underlines the reason for mass schooling. Modern society is, indeed, a schooled society. We will present the main functions of the school system with its universal rules of the institutional organisation subordinated to serve the systemic needs – to prepare citizens, workers and active independent social actors. We will show that, despite different forms of school systems worldwide, the institution of school operates in the same logic of modernity.

Next, we attempt to reconstruct the basic rules of schooling from various sociological perspectives. As a result, we present different ways of analysing school education according to the classical theoretical orientations in the sociology of education: functionalist, conflict and interpretative. We conclude that the full recognition and interpretation of the school system requires a comprehensive approach through the prism of its main features and functions: institutional character, socialisation and allocation.

In the third part of Chapter 2, we propose a comprehensive model of analyses derived from the synthesis of different theoretical approaches. We demonstrate schooling as a sphere conditioned by systemic requirements, however, relatively autonomous according to the logic of operation of each particular school. It is necessary to use both a micro and macro perspective in order to capture the logic of school organisation, its universal character and persistence in time – even in the face of such dramatic events as the experience of distance education during the pandemic. In effect, we propose our analytical model, which enables the interpretation of the phenomenon of schooling and its resistance to change.

Schooled society – The logic of schooling in modern society

Origins of mass education

Education is one of the basic elements of social life these days. The educational expansion observed in the 20th and early 21st centuries has established it as one of the key social institutions. Without a description of the education system and its effects, it is impossible to imagine any meaningful theory explaining the functioning of modern societies today. Education is a focus of interest to almost every discipline of social sciences and humanities, economics or law – from pedagogy, psychology, economics, political science, law and social anthropology, to sociology. Understanding modern society requires looking at the processes taking place in an institution that encompasses the lives of all citizens of developed countries for at least 12 years of their biographies or (for most of them) even longer.

The processes of educational expansion today lead to the formation of the so-called schooled society, in which school performance and career are key activities in a person's life and determine their subsequent life paths (see Baker, 2009a). Therefore, we observe the phenomenon of educationalisation (i.e., the expansion of the forms of school life, especially training tools and procedures, into other spheres of life) (Schaub, 2010; Baker, 2011; Mikiewicz, 2016, Mikiewicz, 2021). Social problems begin to be discussed through the prism of education – in a sense, they become educational problems. Education and its functioning is, on one hand, the culprit of the socio-political status quo. On the other hand, it is the hope for solving social problems.

The functioning of school education, which in the 20th century became an "obvious obviousness", is a natural part of everyone's biography. Everyone went to school at least for a short time (today, one will no longer find people who have not experienced "going to school"). School and school experiences are present in mass culture, where they are a reservoir of natural associations and recognition of life experiences for almost every individual, irrespective of the geographical latitude in which they live. When we watch such productions as *Dead Poets Society*, *Harry Potter*, *The Amazing World of Gumball* or even *Shrek*, it is clear that they include references to associations with school culture, accentuating the obviousness of going to school, where one meets characters such as school actors (students, teachers, principals, etc.). In effect, one could rightly claim that the school experience (the experience of attending a school institution) is the central biographical experience of modern individuals.

For today's members of Western societies, primary and secondary education is a natural part of the biography. Most people spend between 9 and 12 years of compulsory education in school, with various training options depending on the shape of each country's education system. Most countries have clear requirements for primary, secondary and tertiary curricula. It is recognised that schooling at each level contributes significantly to the formation of today's workforce. This is a concern not only for nation-states, but also part of the policies of supranational organisations such as the European Union and the Organisation for Economic Cooperation and Development (OECD). According to Baker (2011), "Widespread education in a post-industrial society creates cultural ideas about new types of knowledge, new types of experts, new definitions of personal success and failure, a new workplace and conception of jobs, and new definitions of intelligence and human talent. At the same time, educational achievement and degree attainment have come to dominate social stratification and social mobility, superseding and delegitimising forms of status attainment left over from the past. The global impact of formal education on post-industrial society has been so extensive that one could argue that mass education is the fundamental social revolution of modernity". (Baker, 2011: 11).

For further analysis, it is worth recalling the origins of mass education and its expansion, which dates back to the 17th century; however, it spread out in full force at the beginning of the 19th century. Thus, we see the coincidence of the emergence of the institution of mass school education with the processes of modernisation (i.e., the emergence of modern industrial society). This is associated with the significant processes of modern rationalisation described by the precursors of sociological thought – Max Weber, Karl Marx, Emile Durkheim. It is pointed out that the emergence of mass education is inextricably linked to, and is even the result of, religious, economic and political processes – as a result of which new principles and ideologies of participation of individuals in a complex social reality are formed, which takes on characteristics significantly different from the previous social formation (i.e., traditional society) (Boli, Ramirez, Meyer, 1985: 146). The concepts that need to be mentioned here are as follows:

- Industrialisation – the spread of industrial production methods, the increase in the percentage of people employed in industry, the standardisation of working hours, the clear division of labour and the accompanying increase in the heterogeneity of society. In short, industry becomes the main sphere of the economy;
- Urbanisation – the process of development of urban settlements, often in connection with the location of industrial centres; the concentration of a large population in cities, increase in the overall share of the urban population; the formation of a specific urban lifestyle;
- Rationalisation – the subordination of the organisation of social, economic and political life to the principles of rational planning; belief in scientific progress and the possibility of developing scientific methods of organising social life; associated with this is the so-called disenchantment of the world – i.e., a shift from explanations of a magical-religious nature towards scientific explanations based on the methods of rapidly developing modern disciplines;
- Bureaucratisation – resulting from rationalisation, the process of the spread of organisations based on the model of bureaucracy, the expansion of the power of officials through the subordination of an increasing sphere of social life to legal regulations and procedures; a specific type of social organisation with clear formal rules, an official hierarchy and formal terms of reference for personnel at various levels;
- Individualisation – the process of the consistent formation of a way of thinking about individuals as independent subjects related to others based on exchange and cooperation based on the social division of labour; this way of thinking replaces collectivism (i.e., seeing individuals as an integral part of certain communities; individuals become responsible for their actions – the concept of intra-control personality appears here, instead of tradition-control personality) (Riesmann, 1996; Collins, 2000, Szacka, 2003; Litak, 2005; Draus, Terlecki, 2006).

Of course, all of the processes indicated here are very complex and subject to extensive analyses conducted in social sciences. Here, we bring them up signally to outline the context for the emergence of the idea of the institution of mass education. The elements indicated above became the basis for developing a model of education to respond to social demand. Here is the emergence of a rational tool for a rational society, established for the systematic, purposeful and effective preparation of community members. Theories of the emergence and expansion of mass education accentuate the need for the emergence of this mass institution – as mass as the family (after all, just as everyone has a family, so does everyone go to school) – which complements and sometimes replaces the family in socialisation tasks.

The economy requires specialised workers, whereas the institutions of a rational bureaucratic state require administrative staff. The division of labour, however, becomes so complex that family upbringing is not enough anymore to prepare individuals for work. In other words, it is not sufficient for individuals to watch their family and neighbours to have an idea of what their future profession might be, or what potential roles they could enter in the labour market. These roles begin to differ significantly from those of previous generations, therefore families and older generations cease to be natural reservoirs of valuable knowledge. Technological advances are invalidating previous wisdom. Increasingly rapid economic changes are tearing apart previous social ties and require new socialisation mechanisms.

According to Floud and Halsey, industrialisation, by accelerating the degree of social change, weakens the relationship between subgroups in the labour division system and, consequently, between individuals and the broader social structure. Industrialisation imposes new burdens on educational institutions – the task of mass instruction, the promotion of scientific and technical development, professional recruitment and social selection. The economy becomes increasingly dominated by research institutions and those engaged in technological innovation, causing the differentiation of educational institutions and their functions. Mainly this becomes so because the educational system occupies a strategic place as a central determinant of society's economic, political, social and cultural character (Floud, Halsey, 1959: 290).

This shows the location of the school education system as a central social subsystem in modern society, the framework of which solidified in the 20th century. The development of industrial technology triggered the need to prepare people to perform relevant jobs in factories. Mass production required mass education of trained workers. At the same time, the development of state administration created a need for educated officials. A society adopting a class structure required a mechanism for filling social positions. With the development of technology and the growth of information, the need for an increasingly elaborate method of knowledge transmission and appropriate selection arises. Education is not only becoming an integral part of the social system, but it is also becoming an increasingly important factor in individual and social development.

Modern society is becoming an "open society" in which the principle of meritocracy prevails – no longer birth and ascribed status, but position achieved is the measure of a person's value. As Kingsley Davis (1966) notes, in complex societies, ascribed status factors (gender, age, family of origin) become elements of the resources an individual uses when competing for achieved status. In such societies, unlike small and homogeneous ones, the need arises to establish an institution responsible for socialisation and selection. It is school – more broadly, the school career – that is one of the primary channels of mobility today.

According to researchers of educational institutions (Meyer, 1977; Collins, 1979; Baker, 2011), education had almost no role in mobility processes in the pre-industrial era. During the late feudal period, only a small proportion of elites were allocated based on university degrees. Even at the beginning of the industrial era, allocation in the social structure was based on such factors as the family of origin, position in the social structure, inheritance of status, marriage, age, gender, religious charisma, training in a guild, patronage, caste or land ownership. The situation began to change radically in the mid-19th century. As researchers show: "Whereas the class position of most Americans in 1840 was almost entirely a function of their ownership of property, a century later educational credentials had become the primary and proximate determinant of class position for most people by virtue of the capacity of educational credentials to regulate access to the occupational structure" (Hogan, 1996, after Baker, 2011: 17).

The cultural heritage and stock of technological knowledge are too rich and important to leave socialisation to primary groups. The institution of organised mass education becomes the second agenda of socialisation, alongside family. The establishment of this type of belief – a value system or ideology – is the basis for the functioning of mass education.

Treating the education system as a rationally planned modern social institution, Boli, Ramirez and Meyer distinguished three basic institutional features that have conditioned the emergence and expansion of all modern educational systems:

1. mass education is institutionally shaped to be universal, standardised and rationalised;
2. mass education is institutionalised to a very high degree at a very high level of social organisation. Mass education was not established as a tool for solving particular local problems or group conflicts but as a general system expressing principles of broad validity;
3. mass education was institutionally established to carry out the socialisation of individuals as central social units.

These constitutive features of education grow out of functional and symbolic needs, underpinned by the dialectical arrangement of community and individual:

> Mass education is produced by the social construction of the main institutions of the rationalised, universalistic worldview that developed in the modern period – the citizen-based nation and state, the new religious outlook, and the economic system rooted in individual action [...]. Mass education arose primarily as a means of transforming individuals into members of these new institutional frames that emerged in Europe after the Middle Ages. The nature of society was redefined; society became a rational, purposive project devoted to achieving the new secular ends of progress and human equality. The project was defined in the new institutional frames to include individual members of society as essential components – loci of sovereignty and loyalty, production and consumption, faith and obedience. Thus, the individual must be made rational, purposive, and empowered to act with autonomy and competence in the new universalistic system [...].
> (Boli, Ramirez, Meyer: 156–157)

Boli, Ramirez and Meyer expand their thought on the production of mass education by providing further explanations:

> In the emerging society built around individual membership, theories of socialisation developed and became central. In the new view, the unformed, the parochial, or even the morally defective child could be moulded in desired ways if its environmental experiences were controlled rationally and purposefully. Such

deliberate socialisation was necessary because all of the virtuous goals of society were increasingly seen as attainable only to the extent that individual members of society embodied the corresponding personal virtues. Because society was held to be essentially a collection of individuals, the success or failure of its effort to realise progress and justice was dependent on the nature of the socialisation experiences encountered by the individual. Such a view – that mass education is part of the effort to construct a universalistic and rationalised society, incorporating individuals and their actions – fits well with the distinctive features of mass education we have noted above. Mass education is too all-encompassing and homogeneous to be explained by the division of labour. It is too highly institutionalised in political and religious collectivities of too broad a purview to be seen as a simple reflection of local interest relations. Finally, it focuses too much on the individual as chooser and actor to be conceived as a simple instrument of passivity and labour control in a differentiated society.

(Boli, Ramirez, Meyer: 156–157)[1]

Such thinking about the social determinants of the emergence and development of mass education corresponds with the diagnosis of Emile Durkheim (1956), who pointed out key aspects of modernisation:

a the deepening differentiation of institutions;
b the specialisation of their activities;
c the autonomisation of their fields of activity;
d the interdependence of activities carried out by different institutions in different fields.

Educational institutions, built according to the principles of rational organisation of social life based on the mechanisms of bureaucratic control, become responsible for preparing members of complex societies based on "organic solidarity" – resulting from sharing common values as opposed to "mechanical solidarity" resulting from assignment to a particular group. The idea of the individual ceases to be strictly tied to a specific social base and becomes abstract and universal. The era of the cult of individual independence and subjectivity begins. Thus, a task arises for the institutions of socialisation to shape the independent individuals so that they will nevertheless be able and willing to co-create the social whole (Moore, 2008). Henceforth, the constant ambivalence between creating conditions for individual development and fitting into social structures and needs will be the primary factor of tension and the basis for ideological disputes over educational solutions.

The development of mass education is, thus, seen here as the result of efforts to create a new, rational individual who, however, individualised, occupying a position in a differentiated and networked system of social roles and positions, is the bearer of a universalist ethic and the adherent of a common core of values that allow for the preservation of social cohesion despite differentiation. In doing so, Boli, Ramirez and Meyer point to two models of education for the construction of the individual:

Model 1: Creation of community members

Education emerges as part of an effort to create properly socialised individuals of a rational society who have the capacity and disposition as workers, innovators, consumers, organisers and committed members of a political community. Setting progress and equality as its goal, this model of education presents it as a process of mass mobilisation that unites individuals into a universal "civic culture". Education generates social movements or the readiness to participate in civil society. Educational solutions are decentralised, so they may differ slightly in different regions of the country but are essentially similar as a result of the unifying nature of civic culture, permeating the thinking of individuals and influencing the way they organise social institutions

Model 2: Creation of members of the nation-state

In this model, education becomes a way to create citizens of the state. It shapes loyalty to the state and acceptance of the obligation to vote, go to war, pay taxes, etc. It also equips citizens with the skills and worldview required to contribute productively to national success. The state promotes mass education to transform individuals into members of the national community and fosters a unified system to build commitment to a common set of goals, symbols and assumptions about appropriate conduct in the social arena.

Therefore, on one hand, the progressive differentiation and complexity of social systems and, on the other, ethical universalisation and individualisation as a requirement for the effectiveness of the modern social system (whether in community form or in nation-state form) have become the driving force behind the spread of mass education around the world. At the same time, it explains the differences in how education systems are organized in different countries – whether they are more civically oriented or state-oriented.[2]

The machinery of educational institutions has become a permanent part of the organisation of societies in all so-called developed countries. It has also consistently covered an increasingly long period of individuals' lives. All over the world, young people are spending more and more time in school. This process is referred to as the expansion of education. Over the course of the 20th century, education became a major social institution. What mechanisms are driving its expansion?

Several parallel factors are pointed out when looking for the mechanisms responsible for educational expansion, not always concurrent in their logic. First of all, the links between education and the economy are pointed out. It is believed that the expansion of education is linked to the needs of the labour market, where technological progress is causing a transition from an industrial society to a knowledge-based economy (Toffler, 1986; Nyhan, 2002). Such economic thinking about education was supported by Gary Becker's (1964) human capital theory, which was developed in the 1960s and 1970s. Educational investment became part of the strategic development of societies' wealth, and neoliberal nomenclature and ideology took over the sphere of discourse about schooling and its importance in society. It can be summarised in the laconic statement that the higher the education citizens have, the more productive society is.

The second mechanism stimulating the development of education at successive levels – ideologically perhaps opposed to the neoliberal impulse – was the idea of democratising access to education for all social strata and groups. Educational expansion was supposed to be a way to reduce inequality and "meritocratise" social allocation processes. In other words, it was not social background but the skills imparted and tested at school that were the basis for recruitment to particular positions in the social structure.

Education at increasingly higher levels was also seen as a tool for creating a civil society or, in other words, political mobilisation. Ralph Dahrendorf considered education to be a necessary condition and a guarantee of democracy and a mature society (see Hadjar, Becker, 2009). Forming civic attitudes and exercising the competence of full and legitimate participation in a democratic society is one of the basic tasks for schools.

The constant intermingling of these three elements leads to the fact that the institution of mass education as we know it today is subject to fluctuations due to the tension between its various functions.

At the same time, these different functions lie at the heart of liberal democracy. As David Labaree (2012) suggests, educational policy attempts to reconcile the three main goals of the educational system's operation:

1 democratic equality, which makes education "produce" subjective citizens;
2 social efficiency, which tells education to prepare productive workers;
3 social mobility, which sees education as a way to maintain or improve one's social position.

Education thus "serves three masters", so to speak, or fulfils the needs of the three sides of social life. The first dimension of education, according to Labaree, corresponds to the political dimension of the functioning of societies and is to act on the efficiency needs of the state system. The second dimension outlined above is the operation of education in response to the needs of employers and taxpayers, who want education to prepare economic actors. The third dimension represents the needs and expectations of consumers of education – families and future workers, who regard education as a tool for acquiring the necessary resources and symbols that will allow them to obtain the greatest possible profits in the future.

As a result, education is seen as both a public and an individual (private) good, securing the interests of the collective and individuals. Education as a public good is a tool for investment in the education of citizens and the quality of the workforce. On the other hand, education as a tool of social mobility is an individual good that benefits only those with certain diplomas – very important currency in the labour market today. As a result, education in a liberal democratic society falls into contradictions.

> [...] it is expected to simultaneously serve politics and the market, promote equality and inequality, construct itself and, as a public and private good at the same time, serve the interests of the general public and individuals. From a political perspective, its structure should be flat, the curriculum universal, access open; economically, its structure should be hierarchical, the curriculum divided into different paths, and access linked to effort. From the perspective of democratic equality and social efficiency, its purpose is to socialise and provide knowledge that is useful to citizens and workers; from the perspective of social mobility, its purpose

is to select and provide credentials that allow access to good jobs, regardless of what one has learned along the way.

(Labaree, 2012: 17)

In effect, education is exposed to constant criticism. This is because it is expected to realise all three aspects, to serve the three parties, yet it is impossible to reconcile the expectations of these three stakeholders. As Labaree writes:

> (...) when we put our liberal-democratic goals before education, we want it to take them all seriously, but we don't want to push any of them too far, because doing so would end up jeopardising the achievement of other, equally valued goals. We expect education to promote social equality, but we want it to do so in a way that does not threaten individual freedom or private interests. We ask it to promote individual opportunity, but we want it to do so in a way that doesn't compromise social integrity or economic efficiency. As a result, the educational system fails miserably in achieving any of its primordial goals.
>
> (Labaree, 2012: 17)

This basis of modern education is probably why mass education has been criticised since its inception. For this reason, it is constantly subject to reform and change to establish a system that will finally meet public expectations. This, in turn, pushes its development and makes it an increasingly important piece of the social puzzle.

Different forms, one logic

Mass education systems were formed based on a similar logic of modernisation related to the rationalisation and individualisation indicated earlier. However, it would be a misconception that education systems are the same in all countries. On the contrary, if we look at how educational institutions are organised around the world, we will notice a multiplicity of formal solutions and an even greater diversity in educational content. The very presentation of the functioning of systems in different countries is an arduous and exciting task simultaneously because it shows the very different backgrounds of the functioning of education in specific social systems.

Yet, educational systems around the world are subject to the same logic. We can consider this as an effect of universalism and institutional convergence. This is also due to the conditions of the emergence of mass education outlined above – in all modern societies, the educational mechanism is based on the same logic of creating "socialised individuals". Although these systems vary in terms of detailed organisational arrangements, the basis is the division into three phases in the educational cycle – elementary (primary education), secondary, tertiary and higher education. To this, we should add the stage of pre-school preparation – preschool, kindergartens and, on the other hand, the increasingly growing segment of doctoral studies.

An expression of the uniformity of educational logic worldwide is the process of monitoring the functioning of education systems and their effects worldwide by international organisations such as the OECD. When comparing systems and their effects, one must assume the symmetry of structures and processes. Moreover, the very fact of international monitoring produces persuasive language that stimulates institutional convergence. An example and, at the same time, expression of this uniformity is the International Standard Classification of Education (ISCED) classification adopted to enable comparability of systems.

Observation of the various systemic solutions related to education around the world shows two seemingly contradictory issues. First, we see a very wide variety of structural solutions in the field of education. In fact, no two education systems in the world are the same. There are as many systems as there are states and, even more so, because federalist states allow different systems to be organised in each member of the federation – the Länder in Germany, the Cantons in Switzerland, the States in Canada and the US. So, a great deal of diversity and uniqueness of individual educational systems is apparent. On the other hand, however, we see similar components in all systems from pre-school education to higher education:

1 in all systems, there are elements of examination and certification of knowledge;
2 in all systems, there is rationalisation and uniformity of education and, more broadly, of socialisation – treating school as the primary channel of intra-generational mobility;
3 in all countries, the sphere of education is subject to control and is seen as one of the key elements determining the economic efficiency of the economy.

The fact that institutions such as the World Bank or the OECD prepare tools for monitoring and evaluating the effectiveness of education systems in different countries stimulates this process of unification of organisational solutions. Annual reports by *Education at Glance* or surveys such as *PISA – Programme for International Student Assessment, PIRLS – Progress in International Reading Literacy Study, TIMMS – Trends in International Mathematics and Science Study* and *TALIS – Teaching and Learning International Survey* contribute to spreading the belief that education worldwide is governed by the same laws and can be described according to the same categories. This, in turn, impacts national governments, which see such comparisons as a good way to determine the effectiveness (quality) of their systemic solutions in the field of education. A kind of ranking of systems is being built – in each country, educational stakeholders get excited about the results of such surveys, either rejoicing at rising in the rankings or distressed at falling or being in low positions. So-called PISA shock is a driving element in education policy in Germany, Belgium, the US, Australia and other countries. Countries that are high in the ranking are analysed in search of reasons for their good performance and become a source of solutions adapted in other systems. This leads to further unification of systems, if not in terms of formal organisational structures, then in terms of the logic of operation.

The mechanisms indicated here show school education as an integral part of modern society and a subject of concern for individual actors (parents and students), governments and transnational systems. This is an important determinant of the logic of school institutions and one of the key reasons for their institutional rigidity (in the organisational and curricular layers). If a certain pattern of institutional arrangements is formed in a given social system, fulfilling the condition of establishing an unstable consensus between the three dimensions of social expectations (political, economic, individual), then we will observe a tendency for these arrangements to persist and any change in this arrangement will give rise to resistance from any of the parties.

Institutionalisation, socialisation and allocation – Mechanisms of schooling from sociological perspectives

In a more limited sense, the word *education* is applied to learning processes carried out at specific times, in specific places outside the family home, for a specific period of time, by people specially prepared or trained for these purposes (Dreeben, 1968: 2).

This classic sentence expresses the essence of how educational institutions function in the modern world. It also points out all the key elements that came under pressure during the COVID-19 crisis and that potentially could have changed under this pressure. In this part of the chapter, we will outline a general analytical model that will allow us to discuss the phenomenon of change (lack of change) in education more formally. We need to reconstruct the basic mechanisms that govern the functioning of this multidimensional social phenomenon: school education. To do this, we need to synthetically recall the basic dimensions of the analysis of school education carried out in sociology. This is difficult because, within the sociological discourse on education, there is a mix of micro-sociological analysis (referring to the language of interaction, role, identity) and macro-sociological analysis (referring to such concepts as system, structure, stratification, etc.). Both of these perspectives should be present in discussing the potential for cultural change in school education.

When trying to define the area of the sociology of education, various classifications are used. According to a classical proposal of Ivan Reid (1978), there is a division into:

- the educational sociology – using sociological knowledge to solve problems in and with education; raising the issue of education as a social problem and attempting practical solutions;
- the sociology of education – sociology here raises questions about the role, functions and operation of education in the broader social system. Here, sociology of education is taken as a sub-discipline of general sociology, like sociology of the family or sociology of the state;
- the sociology of school – the application of various theoretical approaches to depict and understand the daily work of schools.

Reid also states that there are two main theoretical approaches to educational analysis:

- structural, which focuses on the functioning of education from a macro-social perspective, as part of a specific social whole;
- interpretative, which uses an interactional, phenomenological and ethnomethodological perspective to analyse educational institutions and the social worlds that are created in and around them.

Walter Feinberg and Jonas Soltis (2000) present a sociology of education organising the narrative around three theoretical traditions:

- a structural-functional approach emphasising the action of the school to maintain social order, viewing educational institutions as one of the primary institutions for ensuring social solidarity;

- a conflict approach emphasising the contradictions that exist between different social groups, classes and strata, pointing to education as a tool of struggle for interests and an instrument for imposing the domination of one group over others;
- an interpretative approach accentuating the processes of creating specific meanings in the school space and presenting the specific worlds of individual schools.

A similar ordering strategy can be found in another item proposed by Roland Meighan (1993) and in the same vein is maintained the classification of Albert H. Halsey and Jerome Karabel (1977), who point to the functional approach, the conflict approach and the so-called new sociology of education, which attempts to combine the basic findings of the previous two perspectives and supplement them with elements of the interpretative approach and the sociology of knowledge.

Classifications that begin with an overview of the social fields of education's impacts run from a slightly different direction. For example, Aaron Pallas (2000), looking at the impact of education on the lives of individuals, points to three types of explanations for this impact:

1 The first, called the socialisation theory, indicates that schooling transforms individuals' characteristics by providing them with knowledge. By preparing the individual to function in the world of work, institutions and relations of the social world, school shapes their knowledge and ways of using knowledge;
2 According to the second approach, the so-called allocative approach, educational achievement is a reward that allows individuals to access desirable positions that further bring certain tangible and intangible benefits. Educational institutions select individuals for these positions based on their achievements and abilities;
3 The third approach emphasises the influence of schools on individuals through the institutional authority of education, which affects the social structure. According to this approach, education affects society not by changing the quality of individuals or allocating those individuals in the structure, but by transforming the very structure of social institutions – in other words, by having society organise itself in such a way that it allows socialisation and allocation based on educational structures and processes.

The field of sociology of education is similarly characterised by Scott Davies and Neil Guppy (2010), who emphasise the division into three analytical traditions:

1. education as a tool of socialisation – analyses focus on the processes of shaping knowledge, competencies, attitudes and values of educational participants;
2. education as a tool of selection – analyses focus on looking at the opportunities provided by education for individuals and the social inequalities that manifest themselves within it;
3. education as a tool for social organisation and legitimisation of knowledge – an approach that analyses education as a kind of institutional creation that influences other institutions in society.

These authors point out that within each analytical tradition, we are dealing with different theoretical approaches. Thus, when analysing the socialising impact of education, we are dealing with such approaches as:

- structural functionalism, which focuses on analysing the education system's formation of the values and attitudes necessary to maintain the balance of the social system;
- neo-Marxism, which analyses the hidden agenda of school influence as oppressive and imposing attitudes and values on individuals in the name of preserving the dominance of certain interest groups;
- an ascriptive approach, where education is seen as a tool for shaping racial and gender identities;
- reflexive modernisation (or new individualism), where education is viewed as an element that is the result of the formation of a new individualism associated with the super-reflexivity of late modernity, on one hand, and as a tool for dealing with insecurity in a risk society, on the other.

On the other hand, within the approach dealing with the selection or allocative aspects of the functioning of education, we have:

- functional stratification theory, where the mechanisms of a meritocratic society are analysed;
- neo-Marxism, where the analysis deals with the mechanisms limiting vertical mobility through education;

- the analysis of the determinants of educational success, where analysts focus on the variation in the forms of capital available to individuals, primarily in the unequal initial conditions of competition for educational outcomes;
- an ascriptive approach, where the analysis looks at the social division of labour conditioned by race and gender factors.

Finally, within the analysis of education as an institution that organises the social order and legitimises knowledge, we encounter the following thematic bundles:

- human capital theory, treating education as an investment in competencies for the economy and raising an individual's chances in the labour market;
- credentialism, viewing education as the acquisition of status symbols and passes to certain social positions;
- neo-institutionalism, noting that the spread of similar institutional arrangements for education around the world leads to the formation of similar values and social structures – a kind of globalisation through education.

Summarising these different ways of organising the research field of the sociology of education, we can say that the different approaches illuminate three basic issues from a different angle:

1. schools and educational systems are peculiar institutions formed under specific social conditions and influencing their social environment;
2. these institutions have the task of socialising individuals (i.e., forming their attitudes and values in relation to the features of the social structure);
3. these institutions organise, in a certain way, the biographies of individuals by conditioning their allocation in the social structure.

The three dominant theoretical orientations (or paradigms) in sociology – the structural-functional, conflict and interpretative approaches – illuminate a different aspect of each of these issues. For this exact reason, a typology of research problems and interpretative perspectives within the sociology of education has been presented in Table 2.1.

The above table can be read "line by line", indicating how the following topics/problems are discussed in each theoretical approach. We would then analyse how schools as institutions are talked about

Table 2.1 Typology of research problems and interpretive perspectives within the sociology of education

	Theoretical approach		
Theme	Functional	Conflict	Interpretative
Institution	Education as an institution that grows out of the logic of modern society and determines, in turn, the way society is organised	The way education and educational content are organised reflects the prevailing social order and serves to maintain it	School as a social world – a specific arrangement of relationships and meanings, which is built based on the meeting of people in a particular institutional space
Socialisation	Education as a tool for shaping attitudes and values for social sustainability	Education as a tool for creating "false consciousness" and instilling values and norms that legitimise existing social inequalities	Schools as reference groups, places of acquisition of social roles and identity
Allocation	Education as a tool for building a meritocratic society, a space for choices and rational planning by individuals	Education as a mechanism that limits opportunities for social advancement for individuals from lower social strata	Schools as places to build identities related to the envisaged career, social labelling and stimulation of aspirations

Source: (Mikiewicz, 2017: 12, see also Mikiewicz 2016).

in the functional, conflict and interpretive approaches. Similarly, one can present how these orientations see socialisation and, finally, allocation. One can also read this table "column-by-column" and, thus, characterise each theoretical orientation by stating how each of them deals with institutions, socialisation and allocation in and through school. Finally, one can try to talk about each field from this matrix as a separate set of problems addressed by individual researchers posing specific research questions. Each of these fields constitutes a specific area of questions and a repertoire of research approaches.

The most common approach to presenting the analytical field of the sociology of education is to show the specifics of theoretical approaches. This follows the logic of reading the above table "by columns". An extensive discussion of these approaches exceeds the framework of this text. However, it is worth summarising the essence of these three approaches very synthetically to then focus on the problem analysis (i.e., "reading the table by rows"). This is a procedure that, in our opinion, makes it possible to begin work on a synthesising analytical model of the sociology of education in regard to understanding school organisation (cultures of schooling).

The basic features of the structural-functional approach can be summarised by pointing out that schools are a tool for stimulating socialisation – they are supposed to shape the moral community and prepare individuals to function in society. This was the primary task of formal education at the time of its inception, when the foundations of national society in the modern formula were being formed, and complex trans-local communities were replacing the logic of local communities. This logic of the school is the basis for interpreting its activities to this day despite the changed conditions of social organisation. The question addressed here is how schools respond to social change and whether they adequately prepare young people for social realities. Schools are also a tool of allocation – they deploy individuals in the social structure through the mechanism of school selection. The shape of the school structure, possible pathways, selection thresholds and educational choice processes are analysed here. Formal education is responsible for forming social competencies and attitudes, selecting and allocating, regulating the aspirations and motivating students' efforts in the processes of intra-generational mobility. Existing social inequalities in education are treated here as the result of school-independent inequalities of characteristics in the social structure – in the level of intelligence and attitudes towards education or calculations of gains and losses of individuals and their families (see, for example, Durkheim, 1956; Blau, Duncan, 1967; Boudon, 1982; Sorokin, 2009).

Within the framework of conflict-oriented analyses, the general conclusions are that schools are an instrument of oppression and domination. The basis of this oppressive influence is the task of preparing workers for the labour market so that the school is subordinated to the needs of this market. Within this framework, determined by the logic of Marxian theory, the perspective of schools is treated as a tool for maintaining the social domination of certain social groups through the imposition of a certain legitimate culture and a mechanism of symbolic violence. All of this is done to maintain the privileged position of dominant groups in access to socially desirable resources. According to the analyses conducted in this stream, social inequality in education is determined by socialisation mechanisms outside school and the cultural and social resources of families – school selections favour students from the social elite (see, for example, Kwieciński, 1995, 2002; Bowles, Gintis, 2002, 2011; Bourdieu, Passeron, 2011).

In the optics of the interpretive approach, formal education is a specific meeting place of individuals who, in the process of interaction, jointly establish the meanings and senses of school reality using their symbolic resources. The assumptions of symbolic interactionism and phenomenology, pointing to the importance of knowledge and social creation of meanings, form the basis of the analyses carried out. According to this approach, each school is a *de facto* separate social world, built on the mechanism of symbolisation and the creation of cultures within the school. School culture, however unique in each case, is based on certain structured patterns that are subject to ritualisation. The task of sociology is to interpret the meanings produced in school realities and their impact on the actions of individuals in places called schools (see, for example, Jackson, 1968; Woods, 1983; McLaren, 1989; Janowski, 1995).

The different concepts grow out of different theoretical foundations, and research orientations do not necessarily agree in terms of their interpretations of educational mechanisms. There is an evaluative assessment inherent in each of them: structural functionalism rather positively evaluates the role of education in society and provides a background for justifying its solutions, conflict orientation rather negatively considers the role of education in society and provides a background for exposing the hidden (disreputable) functions of schools. The interpretative orientation appears to be neutral in this regard. However, when we look at the applications of the interpretative approach in the sociology of education, we see that the representatives of this current often "gravitate" towards critical pedagogy. Their analyses are subordinated to the "detection" of negative impacts resulting from interactional and symbolic arrangements in schools (see, for example, research on the hidden agenda of schools or the new sociology of education, Meighan, 1993; Pauluk, 2016).

Trying to escape moral judgements and labels, it seems more effective to organise theses on education around three problem fields (or three research traditions – reading Table 2.1 in rows):

- the institutional approach – treating education and schools as bureaucratic social institutions, creating social order;
- the socialisation approach – treating education as a tool for shaping attitudes and values;
- the allocative approach – treating schools and the education system as a tool for introducing individuals to social positions in adult life.

Each of these problem fields can be analysed from different theoretical orientations. The research results can not only lead to value judgements but also give some idea of the social processes involved in the functioning of formal education. To put it differently, a full analysis of the functioning of education systems should include all the aspects indicated here. Theoretical orientations illuminate different aspects of the functioning of education concerning particular problem fields. However, as divergent as they may be in terms of theoretical sources and research methods, each of the highlighted problem fields completes the picture of the operation of education in connection with social structures while showing that the school and education system itself is a social reality governed by specific rules.

Schools as institutions

Schools are institutions that grow out of the logic of social change that occurred during the transition from traditional society to modern society. It is a bureaucratic organisation with trained staff and structured agenda – curriculum. Modernisation is the cultural ideological basis for the functioning of the structure, which was to become a rational means for the formation of rational citizens of states and national societies. It can be figuratively said that school reflects the spirit of its time. On the other hand, these socially regulated structures of socialisation and allocation condition the shape and functioning of other structures – economic and cultural – by producing knowledge and ideologies, equipping individuals with this knowledge and sanctioning their social roles through formal certifications.

Moving to the conflict analyses, we will point out that these institutions co-create and legitimise the existing social order with its specific inequalities and advantages (see, for example, Collins, 1979, 2000). Researchers from this stream criticise the inequalities and injustices of the system's functioning. This does not change the fact that the shape of school institutions always reflects the interest structures and dominant ideologies of the time. In principle, the conflict and functional approaches do not differ in terms of their fundamental findings in this regard. Therefore, suspending the evaluative nature of the claims, we will point out that school institutions reflect the social relations in the social system. This is reflected in the school system's structure and curriculum.

Interpretive optics sheds light on school institutions from a microsocial perspective – individual schools, which, from a formal-legal point of view, are similar bureaucratic institutions seen up close using interactional, phenomenological and ethnomethodological theories, become differentiated worlds. From this perspective, each school is different because it is constructed by subjects equipped with the self and the ability to communicate symbolically. In the daily rituals of interaction, these subjects co-create a school world of meaning that conditions the actions of the individuals who meet in this world. They draw interpretations from the interactional framework and use the resources of knowledge they possess to create patterns for their behaviour and for interacting with others. The uniqueness of school worlds, however, is limited due to the fact that each of those worlds is created by the interpretative tools shaped in the wider social contexts (see Woods, 1983, 1986). On the other hand, any change in the forms of communication in school relationships and the knowledge produced in these interactional practices can provide the impetus for changing the interpretive structures used in broader social arrangements – for example, changes of interactional practices in workplaces based on interactional habits formed in the school experience.

Schools as spaces of socialisation

In structural-functional optics, schools are tools for supplementing and/or replacing families in forming the desired attitudes of members of society. Growing out of the need to form value systems and attitudes that enable the formation and maintenance of social ties with supra-local groups, schools are seen as agencies of preparation for life – both in terms of preparation for occupational roles and in moral terms (see Durkheim, 1956). In this respect, the conflict approach accentuates the socialising action of schools oriented towards preparing individuals for their pre-prescribed places based on social background. It speaks of the formation of a false consciousness for individuals to accept the rules of the social game imposed on them by dominant groups. School legitimises social order by implanting knowledge and beliefs about social relations in such a way that individuals do not deny the existing divisions and rules governing relations in social structures (see, for example, Young, 1971; Apple, 2004). Of course, the conflict approach here differs from the functional approach, but only in the dimension of moral evaluation. The functional approach also emphasises the task of the school as an instrument for instilling knowledge and attitudinal values in such a way as to ensure social conformity.

In the interpretive approach, we descend into the micro-processes that condition the creation of knowledge structures, beliefs and ideologies treated as resources for the action of individuals under the influence of functioning in school relations. The interpretative approach provides tools for the interpretation of the socialisation process – how knowledge structures are created and how school micro-relationships are translated into the identities, attitudes and value hierarchies of individuals.

Schools as a tool of allocation

According to the structural-functional orientation, schools perform allocative functions (i.e., they determine the processes by which individuals occupy target social positions). A school career translates into a professional career, and this determines placement in the system of social stratification. Central to this process is the shape of the school structure and the pathways it determines through the various stages of education. School systems are analysed here in terms of the length of educational pathways, the number of pathways to choose from, the criteria for selection and allocation across pathways, the moments of selection and the mechanisms of transition from the educational period to the occupational phase (see, for example, Kerkhoff, 1995). From a conflict perspective, these processes are analysed in terms of social inequality. The school system, performing allocative functions, privileges some and disadvantages others. Social order is reproduced not only through the mechanisms of socialisation and the instilling of "false consciousness", but also by allocating individuals from different social backgrounds to separate educational pathways (Boudon, 2008; Duru-Belat, 2009). Here, the interpretive approach provides tools to analyse the mechanisms of entry into designated social roles, the processes of social labelling (labelling) (Rosenthal, Jacobson, 1969; Seul, 1991, 1995) and the creation of an identity in accordance with the allocation made through successive passes through selection thresholds (Apple, 2004).

What follows from the argument made above? A full understanding of the functioning of schools and the educational system requires a synthesising approach that can conduct analyses at different levels and dimensions of the functioning of educational systems in their relation to the broader social reality. This is a two-way condition. It is impossible to understand the functioning of education systems in their relation to the macro-level social system without penetrating all three problem dimensions (institution, socialisation, allocation). It requires to look at how schools operate and how the logic of action of individuals, which meets in the specific conditions of the microstructure, is created. On the other hand, it is impossible to understand the logic of the operation of a single school and the dynamics of relations between specific actors in the microstructure without considering all three problem dimensions of the operation of education (institution, socialisation, allocation) and without making reference to the broader social arrangements in which

The comprehensive model of schooling – Synthesis

The considerations in this chapter concern the functioning of educational arrangements – more precisely, school culture – understood as a system of rules governing the behaviour of people who co-create school communities. Thus, this is a topic locating our considerations in a rather micro-sociological perspective. However, as shown so far, it is not possible to consider the mechanisms of individual didactic solutions or the organisation of the work of educational institutions without reference to the broader contexts of the social system. At this point, it is necessary to move on to a description of the logic of the work of schools as central and basic elements of the educational system in modern societies.

The question we pose here is: what determines organisational solutions in the work of schools? The synthetic argument presented above on the determinants of the work of the education system allows us to see individual educational institutions from a dual perspective – on one hand, we focus on single school organisation; on the other hand, it is an element of a broader system. The culture of school, as well as the functioning of individual institutions, is structurally conditioned and thus, to some extent, universal, which could be called the systemic perspective (see Figure 2.1) At the same time, it is relatively autonomous, based on social worlds of meaning in the relationship of teachers and students, which could be interpreted as the micro perspective (see Figure 2.2)

In addition, it is necessary to look at school as a space of intersecting, or overlapping, reasons of action governing its daily life:

- institutional dimension;
- allocative dimension;
- the socialisation dimension.

And the three dimensions of social discourse on education, according to Labaree, are as follows:

- economic;
- state;
- individual.

As a result, a comprehensive model of schooling has been proposed (see Figure 2.3).

56 *School in its essence*

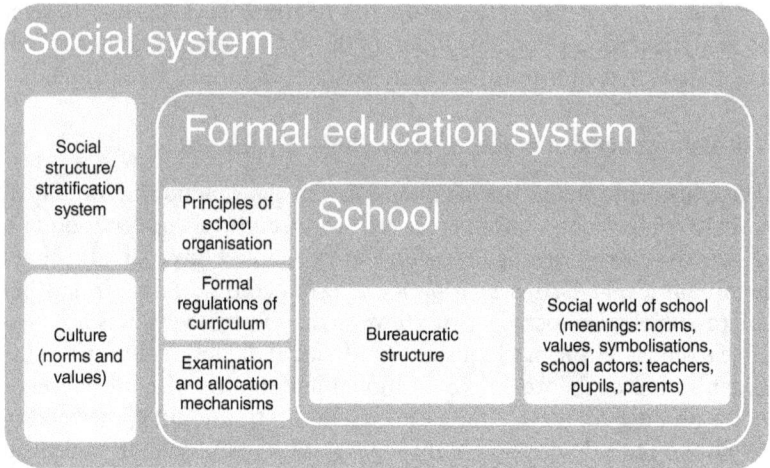

Figure 2.1 The logic of structural conditions of schooling – a systemic perspective

Under such systemic circumstances, the pragmatics of how individual schools function are formed. The everyday grammar of school culture results from systemic conditions. At the same time, it is relatively autonomous; that is, the course of specific interactions within the pedagogical relationship (the relationship between teacher and student)

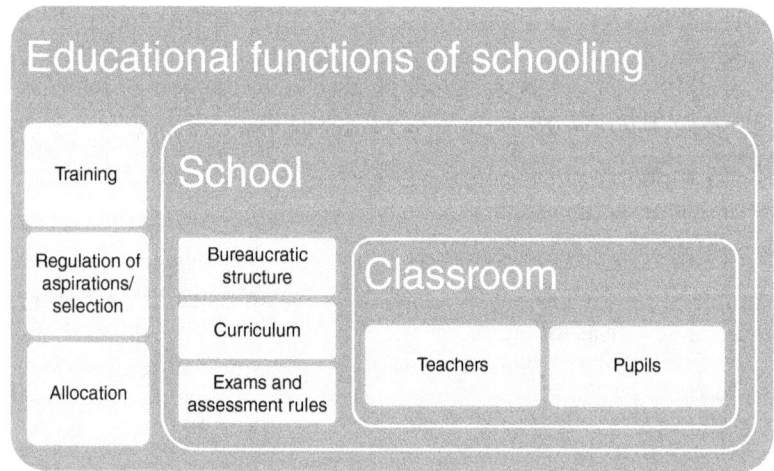

Figure 2.2 The logic of structural conditions of schooling – a micro perspective

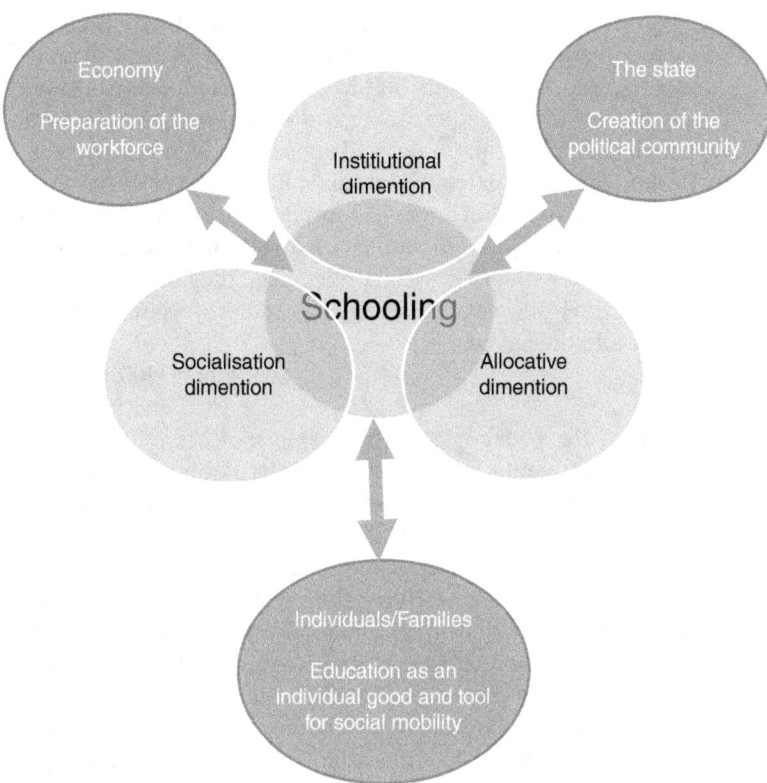

Figure 2.3 A comprehensive model of schooling – synthesis

is determined by factors of a cultural, social and situational nature. However, the pedagogical relationship seems to have a universal character. Regardless of the school system, it is built on the same principles and leads to the production of a bundle of organisational consequences that give final shape to the socio-cultural frame of the school situation.

What defines the nature of the social relationship at school? As Florian Znaniecki writes:

> First of all, the student's social role is different from that of a human individual in any other group. They are not and will not be in such a relationship with anyone outside the school as they are with individual teachers, other students, and the school as a whole. Outside the teacher, there are no individuals whose sole

duty [to him/her] is to teach him and to whom it would be their duty to submit to teaching; there are no individuals outside the student group with whom he/she is connected essentially and solely by learning together; there is no group outside the school in which their participation would consist solely in taking part in collective preparation for future social life. They do learn various things outside of school and will continue to learn in later life, but this learning is always only a part of some other social relations; it is connected with other social duties, as in the family and neighbourhood environment, in the religious and professional group, in the state and the nation.

(Znaniecki, 2001: 182–183)

The essence of the pedagogical relationship (Spiecker, 1984: 203) is, therefore, to make the educational process the basis for defining the roles of the two subjects of this relationship – the student and the teacher. The key role of the teacher (and the educational institution in mass education) is to design this process and to check its effectiveness. Thus, assessment, as the basis for verifying the effectiveness of the teacher's and student's tasks, becomes the basic motive for organising the relationship and organisation of the entire educational system. At the same time, assessment is a micro-level organisational response to systemic expectations – assessment (evaluation of learning outcomes) is the basis of selection and allocation. As Agnieszka Gromkowska-Melosik (2017) pointed out, testing summarises basic functions of schooling – socialisation and selection. Assessment is the basis of social control at school. It is the goal of student performance, the focus of parental interest and the basis for the evaluation of school effectiveness by educational authorities and entire educational systems in cross national comparisons. Surveys like PISA are the "big exam" that countries take every three years, with individuals eager to look for their score in the OECD ranking.

Everything else in the school culture kaleidoscope follows from this base.

We can now present the logic of organising the everyday life of a school as a response to systemic expectations and conditions. The formal education system and each individual school creates the conditions for realising the pedagogical relationship. The nature of this relationship defines tasks and gives a framework for the interaction that builds up around this relationship. Teachers have a task to organise student learning, and this task limits the range of behaviours at their disposal. Similarly, students have a task to learn, which provides an interpretive framework for their actions. The logic of the pedagogical relationship frames (to use Goffman's language) is the interaction between teachers and students.

These roles are not always played smoothly – there is not always agreement on the course of interaction, and not always one and the other want to cooperate. Very often, school situations are a sphere of play between those who want to maintain the definition of the school situation and, therefore, maintain the logic of the pedagogical relationship and those who try to escape from this logic to undermine the definition of the situation or disrupt the relationship. This was very vividly described by Paul Willis (1977) in describing the struggles of school staff against the school resistance of working-class boys. Similarly, Peter McLaren (1986) portrayed the struggle between the school institution and students in Catholic schools in Canada (see also Mikiewicz, 2005 on the culture of resistance in vocational schools in Poland). However, regardless of the attempts observed worldwide and in every educational system to contest the course of the school game, it will be noted that it is built around the logic of this basic relationship between the teacher and the learner.

The very shape of school relations is potentially unique in each institution because of the mechanisms for establishing meanings between the actors who meet there. After all, students and teachers bring [to schools] specific ways of symbolisation based on their habitus and stock of cultural capital (to speak Bourdieu's language). In theory, it is possible to imagine a different course of school relations each time. Yet, paradoxically, these relationships look similar all over the world. Why?

The concept of structuration proposed by Anthony Giddens (1984) provides tools for understanding this persistence. He proposes an alternative understanding of social structure, not as an objective arrangement of positions and relations between positions, but as rules and resources that individuals use in their actions. Rules are generalised procedures that actors understand and use in different circumstances. It is often an unconscious technique or prescription for actions that:

1 are often used in conversations, interaction rituals and daily routines [of the individual];
2 have been tacitly grasped and understood;
3 remain informal, unrecorded and inarticulate.

Resources, in turn, are the kind of facilities that serve actors in their activities. In addition to knowledge of the rules of action, there must also be the ability to implement the action (i.e., material equipment and organisational capabilities). Rules and resources co-create the social structure (i.e., what the actors use); it is not some external reality that pushes and directs the actors. Social structures are rules and resources that can be transformed when actors use them in specific circumstances. Structures are then not so much there as they become when actors use rules and resources in specific situations. Social structure remains susceptible to distortion and is flexible, being "part" of the actors in specific situations and used by them to create patterns of social relations over time and space. This shows the conventional nature of social order and the practically ubiquitous nature of constant transformation whenever someone fails to apply a rule according to the existing pattern. So, how is social order possible?

The institutionalisation of structures in place and time (i.e., the petrification and repetition of patterns of action) requires the routinisation and regionalisation of interactions. Routinisation of interaction patterns ensures their continuity over time, thus reproducing the structure (rules and resources). It also introduces an element of predictability which provides a sense of ontological security. Routinisation includes:

1 opening and closing rituals – ways of communicating the start and end of interactions;
2 observance of order in conversation;
3 tact – a tacit agreement between participants in an interaction about how to behave in given circumstances and how to respond to what would be appropriate and what would be inappropriate;
4 positioning – people bring their positions (roles) to the situation, giving them certain powers and obligations;
5 framing – each institution runs within a certain contextual framework that provides formulas for interpretation, so they maintain consistency of interaction.

Regionalisation, on the other hand, organises action in space by deploying actors in interdependent locations and by specifying how they are to present themselves and act. It is based on specific scenery design – certain physical spaces are linked to specific action structures. They provide contextual interpretive resources: what is supposed to happen in that space. Social structures, as resources and rules of action, are perpetuated through their schematisation ritualised and embedded in specific locations and symbolically organised spaces.

As researchers representing the conflict perspective point out, the school and the classroom are battlefields for meanings for the definition of situations and the logic of action. Two basic groups clash: teachers as representatives of power and institutions, and students as objects of oppression. However, students are not completely defenceless as they can fight to appropriate the school space with their own alternative symbols. In this regard, Peter McLaren refers to Victor Turner's concept of ritual and social games, which treats society as a process in which meanings are continually produced in relationships between individuals. Victor Turner (2005) treats structure as a quality induced and maintained by ritual. Structure imposes a particular pattern of roles and positions and assigns tasks and positions individuals in mutual relationships. This is done through symbolic ritual operations, gestures, words and sequences of events. The opposite of structure is "anti-structure", a state of complete union outside norms and regulations, a state of freedom and unity, described by the term *communitas* (which could be associated with the concept of community). Anti-structure is a liminal state of liberation from rules, a state beyond norms and structures.

Social reality is constant tension between structure and anti-structure – an imposed order of positions and relationships and a spontaneous state of unification in the *communitas*. School reality is tension between the educational structure produced and reproduced in school rituals and a state of liberation from its rules, of freedom outside the structure in the sense of *communitas*. The anti-structure of resistance described by McLaren is the means taken by students to break the order imposed by the school.

Ritual as a sequence of repetitive and symbolically saturated behaviour is central to the creation of social order. The specific order of interaction, the sequence of events and the rules governing the relationship between interaction partners are determined by the ritualistic course of the encounter. Peter McLaren highlights the following functions of ritual:

a   ritual provides an interpretive framework for the course of interaction;
b   ritual determines the holistic symbolic scope of the interaction – it creates reality;
c   ritual communicates by classifying information in different contexts;
d   ritual transforms its participants into certain statuses and certain states of consciousness;
e   ritual defines and articulates meanings through meaningful rhythm;
f   ritual introduces an aura of sacredness and the presence of supernatural powers;

g participation in rituals provides participants with unique knowledge;
h the language of ritual has performative power – it produces real effects;
i rituals reify the socio-cultural worlds in which they are rooted;
j ritual can invert the norms and values of the dominant social order;
k ritual enables participants to reflect on their own interpretive processes as well as their position in the dominant culture;
l rituals have a political aspect and can serve to transmit ideologies and worldviews;
m rituals have the ability to unite opposing areas of experience such as the physical and the moral.

Summarising various conceptions of the meaning of ritual in social life, McLaren offers a synthetic definition of ritual:

> Ritualisation is a process that includes the embodiment of symbols, sets of symbols, metaphors and ingrained patterns through formative bodily gestures. As forms of established meaning, rituals enable social actors to define, negotiate and articulate their phenomenological existence as social, cultural and moral beings.
> (1986: 48)

To put it somewhat simplistically, rituals create the world in which we act in that they define us as participants in that world by giving us certain positions and, therefore, giving us opportunities to act in relation to other people. Just as a religious ritual creates the reality of worship, defining the priests and ordinary believers, school rituals create the reality of education and define its actors – students and teachers. Rituals remind everyone who they are, where they are and why they are there. They recreate logic, impose meanings and organise impressions. The guards of the ritual control are its participants. Resistance to power and domination requires rejecting rituals and, in its extreme form, proposing one's own rituals to impose one's definition of the situation.[3]

Peter McLaren points out several ritual dimensions in school reality:

1 micro-rituals of lessons;
2 macro-rituals – the entirety of a lesson within a day, including the situation between lessons (breaks) and before and after the end of the lesson;

3   rituals of revitalisation – processual events to maintain engagement and motivation – for example, school board meetings, talks between teachers and students during lessons, academies in honour of a patron;
4   rituals of intensification are a subtype of the ritual of revitalisation and are aimed at maintaining the emotional commitment of students and teachers;
5   rituals of resistance – a series of both subtle and dramatic cultural forms aimed at symbolic inversion and reversal of meanings imposed through forms of domination by teachers and education. In a sense, this is a ceremony of destruction – these are rituals of conflict between students and teachers.

It is not without significance that this ritual reality of school events takes place in relative (or total) isolation. As Florian Znaniecki pointed out:

> A typical school during school hours is a monastery to which no sounds of the outside world come, nothing that could distract the attention of the pupils or educators from the activities that its social content constitutes.
>
> (Znaniecki, 2001: 180–181)

The school is an isolated and enclosed area, sanctified by the fact that young people are preparing for adult roles on the premises. The school becomes a separate social reality through such isolation and subordination of a student's life (at least to the extent that his/her life is spent at school) to the rhythm of training requirements. However, as we have been trying to show since the beginning of this analysis, it is not completely separate. It can be said to be characterised by relative autonomy as it creates the conditions for the creation of separate micro-worlds of unique events between those particular individuals who meet at a particular school. In this respect, the social world and culture of a school's community in London is quite different from that of a school in Wroclaw (in fact two schools in London will be separate social worlds). However, each school is subject to processes of routinisation (ritualisation) and regionalisation (the specifics of space arrangements recalling what the functions of education are) subordinated to a similar logic. On one hand, this organisational logic stems from the very nature of the pedagogical relationship – the teacher's relationship with the learner. On the other hand, it is shaped by systemic expectations – the overlapping systemic dimensions of the state, the economy and the individual needs of citizens – as well as institutional, socialisation and allocative logic. In other words, the processes of routinisation and regionalisation that secure and encase the realisation of the pedagogical relationship arise from the need to simultaneously carry out socialisation and allocation of tasks within the bureaucratised, institutionalised framework of the formal organisation, which is supposed to ensure that the needs of the state, the economy and each citizen are met.

In summary:

1. the implementation of the task of preparing citizens, workers and self-determined individuals takes place in the system of the institutionalised process of training in places called schools;
2. in these places, the formation of specific structures for defining the tasks of participants in this world takes place based on the logic of the pedagogical relationship;
3. the implementation of this relationship is subject to considerations arising from the nature of the pedagogical relationship itself as well as from systemic expectations;
4. these systemic expectations are to secure the realisation of the unstable balance between the needs of the state, the economy and individual units (families);
5. the persistence of the determinants underpinning the pedagogical relationship at school is ensured by the mechanisms of regionalisation and routinisation (ritualisation).

This model shows the interconnectedness of the macro-social system with the organisational arrangements of individual educational institutions. This is a two-way relationship. On one hand, changes in the organisation of school life will occur only if the expectations of the system change. On the other hand, changes in the way the pedagogical relationship is implemented (changes in the interactional rules of the relationship between learners and teachers) can result in changes in the functioning of the social system.

Here, in turn, it is necessary to note that if we consider the systemic change, *de facto*, we are not talking about a change in the expectations of the social system – in other words, it is difficult to expect a rationally organised modern society not to want to secure three basic functions at the system level: the training of citizens, workers for the economy and the realisation of the philosophy of individual subjectivity. Only the definitions regarding being a citizen, worker or subject are changing. After all, we are observing a change in competence requirements in the modern labour market. However, this does not mean that the logic of organising the education system around the pedagogical relationship is negated as a result. One only defines differently the effects of the implementation of this relationship. The responsibility for carrying out this task, however, is always on the side of the institution and its staff. The effectiveness of this task is checked by measuring the effects of education – thus, we return to the importance of assessment.

Assessment of educational results is the axis of school work. This is due to the essence of the pedagogical relationship – its purpose is the implementation of the educational process, which is expected to lead to certain effects in the form of a change in the characteristics of the learner (e.g., an increase in their knowledge, the acquisition of technical skills, a change in attitudes, the acquisition of plotted values). Measuring the effects of this process, of course, take very different forms – from the learner's self-assessment, through subjective observations and teacher evaluations to standardised external tests. In accordance with the logic of the rationalisation of modern society – wishing, on one hand, to satisfy the expectations of the state and economic system and, at the same time, give a sense of fair competition to individuals for whom the education system is a tool for achieving socio-economic status – we are observing tendencies towards standardisation of assessment all over the world. External examinations in Poland and the GCSE exam in the UK are manifestations of this logic. Thus, the goal of the work of teachers and educational institutions becomes the preparation of students for the exam. In turn, the task of the entire school system is to prepare procedures and tools for examinations that will (again, let's repeat this) meet the requirements of the political and economic system and the expectations of individuals.

The ideological basis for the functioning of this system is the principle of meritocracy and democratisation of access. The principle of meritocracy defines the principle of allocating social rewards based on an assessment of an individual's skills and aptitude – the better they are, the more they deserve. The principle of democratisation of access defines the possibility (at least potentially) of equal participation in the race for social rewards regardless of initial social status.

This principle of "contest mobility" (Turner, 1971) dictates the logic of the organisation of the work of schools, which (at least in theory) are supposed to be a tool for levelling initial social inequalities. In other words, the principles of organising the implementation of the pedagogical relationship in schools are supposed to simultaneously promote the best possible organisation of learning processes following system needs while guaranteeing equality of potential opportunities for all. But the element of assessment is indelible, with its core result – selection and allocation to different biographical paths. These processes are institutionalised in form of mechanisms of credentialism, that is, the need for formal certification of skills possessed. All this means that the main mechanisms of control of educational processes are devoted to assessing and checking the effects of learning (teaching). Let's say this is both about the mechanisms (rituals) of control in individual schools and in the institutional school system. The intra-school grading system, the subject expectations of individual teachers, the rules of intra-school selection and the rules of final examinations – as well as preliminary examinations for subsequent stages of education – are the essence of the work of the school system.

Thus, we can complete the model of the formation of school culture patterns with the following statements:

6 assessment and grading are the natural consequence of the implementation of the pedagogical relationship as the basic control disposition of the effects of its implementation;
7 grading is both a function of the pedagogical relationship and the fulfilment of the requirements of the system – politically, economically and individually;
8 the task of the education system is to organise the structures and tools of assessment;
9 grading (assessment) becomes a basic control ritual and sets the tone for patterns of interaction in school – it is subject to routinisation.

Finally, it is necessary to return to the importance of school as a physical place where students and teachers (as well as other participants in the school world) meet. School education happens precisely in concrete places. School is a framework for people, who meet in a specific space. This space is highly structured and, interestingly, looks very similar in every corner of the world. Phil Jackson points out that the specificity of the place resembles the impression given by the interior of a church. This is not about how classrooms are organised in the same way as the church naves, but about the obviousness of association and recognition of where one is.

> No one who enters any of these places would think he was in a guest room or a grocery store or a train station. Even if he enters

there in the middle of the night or at a time when the activities of the people in the place do not indicate its function, he would have no trouble understanding what should be going on here.

(Jackson, 1968: 6)

This phrase, written in the 1960s and describing the cultural reality of the US, seems to be entirely relevant in the 21st century in most countries that implement mass education. It is the place that dictates the definition of a situation, regionalises interactions and imposes a frame for interpreting behaviour (see Giddens, Goffman). Schools worldwide similarly arrange space to organise the experiences of students and teachers.

It is a place equipped with specific objects, instruments and teaching aids. It is filled with specific smells – chalk dust, sweat in the PE hall and smells from the school cafeteria. It's a space so overwhelming that when parents come to parents' evenings, they momentarily step into the roles of students and docilely wait their turn to be questioned by the teacher. In each of us, there are habits and reflexes imprinted by school experiences which reveal themselves unconsciously and automatically, as soon as we experience the trigger for these specific associations (e.g., entering the school corridor or taking a seat on a bench).

It is in this space that the socialisation process takes place and "education happens" (i.e., the dynamic of the pedagogical relationship). "School is a place where exams are passed and failed, where assumed things happen, where new points of view are learned and skills are acquired. But it is also where people sit, listen, wait, raise their hands, shake papers, stand in line, sharpen pencils. School is where we meet friends and enemies, where imagination is unleashed and disagreements arise. But it's also where you stifle a yawn and scratch your initials on the bench top, where you collect money for milk and form queues during breaks. Both aspects of school life, the celebrated one and the unnoticed one, are familiar to all of us, but the latter – even if by its characteristics neglected – seems to deserve more attention from those interested in education". (Jackson, 1968: 3)

The key point here is the observation that the experience of school life is made up of small things – situations that, in their sheer volume, merge into a few juicy memories but, in the everydayness of school life, carry with them the specific experience of being at school. This experience for Jackson primarily involves three factors:

a   the amount of time spent in school;
b   the standardisation of schools and classrooms as a place;
c   the compulsiveness of daily participation.

School takes up a lot of our time; we spend a third of our lives in it. During this time, numerous micro-situations happen, organised around people meeting each other in a specific space. School is compulsory. Compulsory schooling forces us to be in this institution even if we don't particularly enjoy it. Forced to participate in this space, we are subjected to daily ritualistic patterns – a similar order of the day, an order of lessons with opening and closing rituals (with other students of a similar age located in a similar situation and subjected to control by those in authority – the teachers). A school is a crowded and noisy place. It's in constant contact with other people and is exposed to other people's evaluations. It's formal and informal assessments, it's scrutiny from teachers and expectations from peers. It's a complex world of meanings created through contact with other people.

A student encounters a whole set of rules at school that they have to adapt to and cope with. According to Peter Woods (1983), we can point to:

1. rules related to time;
2. rules related to conduct;
3. rules related to the programme;
4. private rules of individual teachers.

The result of this matching is a specific attitude: a whole series of habits that, first, allow one to find oneself in subsequent stages of education and, second, that translate into ways of acting in professional work (where one also has to fit into a certain set of rules and expectations – no longer teachers, but employers and superiors; no longer other students, but colleagues).

Being at school is, therefore, a specific set of events and experiences. Some of them grow out of the official programme of the school institution and some of them happen in passing, inadvertently, so to speak. They are, however, equally important for our functioning here and now and in the future as adults in various roles – employees, parents and citizens. Some call it a "hidden curriculum". In a sense, it is synonymous with the term socialisation. In essence, the designator of this term is the totality of processes that form the attitudes, values and ways of perceiving the world of individuals that take place while they are in school. The result of this process is identity, habitus, personality and other psychological terms that we connote with the process of socialisation – at least in terms of the sociology of knowledge proposed by Peter Berger and Thomas Luckmann (2010).

"The hidden curriculum is what is taught by being in school and not by the teacher. No matter how light the teaching staff is, how progressive the programme is, or how community-oriented the school is, something reaches the students that is never talked about in the obvious language lessons or in the prayers at school assemblies. Students pick up a certain approach to life and a certain attitude to learning" (Head, 1974, after Meighan, 1993: 71).

In research practice, it has become accepted to distinguish different dimensions of the impact of the hidden programme or even hidden programmes. Andrew Janowski distinguishes between the hidden programme of textbooks and the hidden programme of everyday school life. Roland Meighan distinguishes several dimensions:

a   the hidden programme of space – the impact of the way the classrooms are organised, the interior of the school, the space around the school, the principal's office, the teachers' room, etc.;
b   the hidden agenda of classroom organisation – the sociology of time at school, the impact of the way classes are organised, the rhythm of lessons and breaks, bells, etc.;
c   hidden aspects of the official curriculum – content secretly smuggled in textbooks, gender stereotypes, biased coverage of history, choice of school readings;
d   the hidden agenda of school organisation – the hierarchy of authority, the management styles implemented by the management, the bureaucratic structures to which both teachers and students are subjected;
e   the hidden agenda of teacher expectations – labelling, gender stereotypes and prejudices about particular social categories, teachers' beliefs about what their charges are capable of learning;
f   the hidden agenda of language – the meaning of linguistic forms present in school, the valuing of formal language, the specificity of texts in textbooks and exercise books, etc.;
g   the hidden agenda of assessment, testing and examination – the importance of subjecting students to assessment, examination mechanisms, the importance of assessment for future school and social careers.

In the context of the considerations carried out in this text, it is important to point out that all these elements are constitutional for the socialisation meaning of school. At the same time, we remember that socialisation tasks are subordinated to three systemic dimensions (economic requirements, political requirements and the creation of subjective individuals). The experience of being in a school environment is one of the primary experiences in the process of secondary socialisation (Berger, Luckmann, 2010), both because of exposure to the factors of the hidden agenda, as well as through participation in the reference groups formed among peers who meet in the institution. In short, it is "going to school" and being in a particular social environment created in a particular physical location that is the fundamental socialisation experience that significantly conditions the biographies of individuals. In this social experience, attitudes towards education and towards one's own future are created – plans and aspirations and concrete decisions related to career choices. This is not just a rational calculation, but also the result of socialisation in a particular social environment. Hence, for many parents, just as important as the educational programme offered or the quality of the staff – if not more important in choosing a school – is the issue of the social composition of the institution (see Ball, 2003). Thus, we can point out the last element of the analytical model:

10 the importance of physical co-presence and the hidden curriculum of the school – all processes of shaping pedagogical relations in terms of serving the systemic needs of the society happens in the physical settings of school settlement.

Conclusion

Analyses presented above lead to the conclusion that permanence of the school culture is rooted in the logic of the pedagogical relation. Together with the rituals of grading, the nature of pedagogical relation determines the other interaction rituals in the school space. The functioning of this relation is relatively autonomous, built on the basis of the dynamics of the interaction between students and teachers. Yet, the structural conditions of pedagogical relations in each school are the outcome of the systemic needs of the social system. School education always serves to build the balance between contradictory expectations of the state, economy and individuals. The essence of schooling is socialisation and allocation in the institutionalised form. The systemic logic of schooling results in the institutionalised forms of organisation of educational relations by rules of routinisation and regionalisation. Schooling is framed similarly in all modern societies and supplies the system with citizens, workers and individual subjects crafted according to the logic of modernity.

Real transformation of education system would require significant changes, first of all, in the logic of pedagogical relation and subsequently in the mechanisms of assessment. Changes in this mechanism would require a redefinition of the systemic expectations towards schooling. On another note, possible radical changes in this mechanism (the implementation of the pedagogical relationship and grading as its most important elements) could bring significant changes to the logic of the social system's functioning.

The situation of the COVID-19 crisis has become an opportunity to identify these mechanisms more clearly than before. Was the experience of the distance education a turning point in the organisation of schooling? Let us try to discuss this issue in Chapter 3.

Notes

1. It can be associated with the concept of the colonisation of the Life-World by the system proposed by Jurgen Habermas (1984, see also Baxter, 1987; Fleming, 2002).
2. We can note a basic difference in the way education is organised in the countries of the so-called "Old World" (i.e., Europe, and the so-called "New World" – the US, Canada, Australia). The former seem to be based more on the state model, the latter on the community model.
3. For McLaren, school is an oppressive force for students. Oppression in school is primarily about ritual coercion. This oppression, however, is not total. The full operation of ritual requires believers – it requires participation in rituals and ritual patterns with full faith. There is room for resistance and struggle – resistance begins when the official ritual course of events is rejected.

3 Potential direction of change looking forward

Introduction

The conceptual model of schooling presented in the previous theoretical chapter allows us to reflect more analytically on what actually happened during the COVID-19 crisis. Chapter 3 provides the reader with an interpretation of the experiences of distance education explored in Chapter 1 using an analytical model presented in Chapter 2, gradually building up the narrative. We endeavour to illustrate how different aspects of schooling and issues that occurred during the coronavirus pandemic can be understood as a two-fold struggle; first of all, to sustain the logic of the pedagogical relationship in school; second, to fulfil the systemic tasks of schooling – socialisation and allocation. In this chapter, we explain why the predicted and – to some extent – expected change in educational culture did not happen because of the logic of schooling.

In addition, we attempt to deploy elements of future thinking, raising questions about potential directions of change:

1. Questions about institutional changes – can distance education become a catalyst for reorganising patterns of the organisation of schooling?
2. Questions about socialisation – can distance education change the mechanisms of acquiring skills and personal traits?
3. Questions about allocation – can distance education change selection and social mobility patterns?

The answers are inconclusive and preliminary; therefore, they open up new fields of discussion about the need and potential direction of change in the school culture.

Potential direction of change looking forward 73

What happened – An interpretation of the crisis

In summary, the challenges that education systems around the world had to face, according to our analytical model, are three-fold:

- the adaptation of the bureaucratic institution to different working conditions;
- dilemmas with regard to selection and allocation processes based on school performance;
- the socialisation function of the school institution supporting (or replacing) families in introducing pupils into their future social positions as young adults.

These are interrelated processes which overlap in the reality of schooling and take place thanks to the most fundamental element of any education system – the pedagogical relationship. The latter constitutes the logic of the relationship between teachers and pupils, as well as the organisation of educational solutions. This social relationship, embedded in the educational practice based on ritualisation and regionalisation, takes place in unique environments called schools at a clearly defined time (school classes), where teachers and students meet to enact their roles.

The pandemic uprooted the school institution overnight from its framework, based on physical presence in the school buildings and filled with ritual activities. This meant the reorganisation of the rules of the pedagogical relationship due to new, digital circumstances, without routines and, above all, without space. Consequently, this very relationship needed a new interactional repertoire.

In the absence of direct contact between teachers and students, the key issue turned out to be the lack of appropriate tools for controlling the pedagogical relationship in education, as well as the definition of the school actors in the new reality of school.

How do you build a repertoire of teacher and student roles?

First and foremost, teachers had to navigate their way in the new communication mode of virtual reality, resulting in indirect interactions with students. When adopting a synchronous distance education model, this meant they had to learn to proficiently use communication technologies to master content delivery, as well as to manage time efficiently. Likewise, students learned (from scratch) how to participate in online classes, how much flexibility and freedom they had due to teachers' lack of control over their behaviour and, finally, what tactics they could use "to survive" and receive the desired grade.

In the case of the asynchronous education model, this meant a completely new definition of roles, where the teacher's actions were limited to defining the content of learning for pupils, followed by the activities to be worked through. The students could work at their own pace, according to their own approach to time management. The social relationship in such a model implies the involvement of each party without the stimulating factor of the physical presence of the other party in the pedagogical relationship. While in the synchronous model we can talk about the possibility of playing out ritualistic school roles in quasi-direct contact between teachers and students (after all, it is just like in a school classroom, but in an online setting), in the asynchronous model this possibility disappears. As previously stated, ritual performance is fundamental to the (re)production of the universe of meanings that defines the lived worlds of individuals – in this case, school teachers and students – because it defines their roles, as well as the rules of their performance on the school stage.

How do you monitor compliance with the norm of pedagogical relationship and motivate the parties to perform their roles accordingly?

Reflecting on the purpose of school rituals, one could simply state that they are tools for stimulating the "expected" behaviours of both pupils and teachers in school. For example, at the beginning of each school day, teachers always complete the registration form – it is a chance to greet their students and start off the school day. Furthermore, at least once a week, teachers and pupils gather together to take part in a school assembly, usually run by the headteacher, during which pupils are expected to sit on the floor/on chairs in a straight line, keep perfectly quiet and listen to what their principal has to say. These are ritual events which recall the definition of the school situation because they remind pupils, as well as teachers, where they are, what their role is and how they are meant to behave in this theatre called school(ing) (Goffman, 1990). It is not surprising that learning remotely from home changes – in fact, undermines – the definition of the school situation due to the fact that the school setting is replaced by pupils' home environment.

In the face-to-face education model, teachers motivate themselves by getting ready for physical interaction with a group, construct tactics for presenting content and use effective strategies for maintaining contact, like an actor in a theatre reacting to the audience's responses and adjusting the presentation of educational content to the observed level of students' understanding of the material. This is again helped by physical co-presence and the use of body language, enabling both teachers and students to pick up non-verbal cues. According to Thomas's role theory, role-playing entails identity – which results in behavioural self-monitoring and provides a system of motivation for action. Similarly, students enter their roles by sitting at their desks, often dressing appropriately for school (uniforms, neat attire, etc.), which, in effect, enhances their motivation by being "in role". In addition, the presence of the rest of the class, the physically co-present peers, confirms the definition of the school situation.

Working in the synchronous distance education model, teachers may have often felt watched by their students, especially if they did not turn on their camera (which happened quite often during the pandemic, particularly amongst older pupils). In this configuration, the pressure on students, with regard to certain types of behaviour prompted by school rituals, disappears completely. Being in an indirect contact, often without vision, students did not feel the need to carry out their typical school behaviour repertoire. Why wear a uniform when no one can see you? They could even be wearing their pyjamas if they wanted to.

As the research reports show, students – especially older ones – have been engaged in various unrelated activities while participating in remote classes, such as chatting with friends, gaming, watching TV, helping parents, etc. As a result, teachers were losing contact with their "audience", often being unaware of students' non-verbal reactions and, hence, assuming rather than knowing that their input was received with understanding. In effect, having a very limited repertoire of behaviours in their performance, teachers' motivation during distance teaching weakened and, ultimately, declined during the pandemic.

The asynchronous model of distance education, where there is not even a single moment of the illusion of co-presence during the online connection, seems to be even more dispiriting for teachers, who act only as facilitators without having to teach "live". In this instance, teachers needed to be motivated to do completely different things – preparing materials on educational platforms, developing activities, checking written work, etc. Students, on the other hand, did not have to participate in school drama, in lesson rituals, and were not subject to the direct control of the teacher and other students (before whom they would not want to be ridiculed in their physical presence).

They had to rely on intrinsic motivation, on the awareness of the importance of education and self-control. They had to work on organising and managing their time, planning to complete tasks given by teachers as well as independently selecting material. In other words, they had to have the will to do it on their own. Control by institutions was present, if only by setting deadlines for handing in written work, but it was not as tangible and oppressive as the in-person school setting.

The issue with the pedagogical relationship and the motivation for teaching and learning during distance education leads to challenges on the organisational level of school performance, such as assessment and exams. The assessment takes place on the individual (teacher-student) level, the macro level of the school – when the rules for classifying students into subsequent years of education had to be adjusted – and at the systemic level, where there is a need to define the rules of formal selection of pupils at the end of each educational stage (i.e., the transition between primary and secondary education and then higher education).

Assessment is a core ritual in school(ing). At the same time, it is the link through which the systemic tasks of education (selection for occupational roles) are connected to the logic of the operation of the pedagogical relationship. School assessment is a verification tool prepared by the institutional system for the rational allocation of individuals to professional tasks and accompanying status rewards according to the logic of meritocracy. At the same time, in the micro dimension of the pedagogical relationship, it is a tool for invoking the power of the teacher and indirectly recalling the principles of the pedagogical relationship. It is the "last instance", the last weapon teachers have to remind students why they are in this relationship and who is in charge.

Hence, as we demonstrated in Chapter 1, assessment – especially the processes of external examinations and grading – was a particularly urgent problem in public discourse. At the same time, for teachers, it was a tool for maintaining the definition of the pedagogical relationship. As observed during the distance education model, the frequency of messages from teachers about pupils' work and behaviour being graded – or in other education systems, simply praised with smiley faces, house points, etc. or disciplined with verbal warnings – was significantly higher comparing to in-person teaching (Mikiewicz et al., 2022).

The issue of grading and examination reveals the institutional dimension of the education system; the rules of grading and selection at subsequent educational stages are subject to bureaucratic regulations that are formal and systemic at the same time. Furthermore, they apply to all institutions in a given school system. As we demonstrated in Chapter 1, governments had to interfere with the logic of grading and selection processes, but without negating this logic in its principle. The reason behind it is straightforward – grading and formal selections are the essence of the allocation processes that education is responsible for.

To what extent do the processes of selection and allocation fulfil their function in the situation of distance education?

In order to answer this question, we need to find out whether schools were able to effectively prepare their pupils to pass their exams and assessments. As shown in Chapter 1, the study shows that the efficiency and effectiveness of distance education in terms of pupils' attainment were lower compared to traditional, in-person education.

The exemplification of this status quo and the frame of reference are the cases of Poland and the UK, in which we observed different institutional responses. In Poland, the mechanism of external exams during the pandemic operated in line with the "usual rules", with a slight adjustment of the timing of external exams. It was changed in order to give students extra time to revise. In the UK, however, it was deemed necessary to modify the process to a greater extent, which – in effect – meant abandoning exam procedures in favour of assessment based on teacher judgement, as well as assessment algorithms. Nevertheless, the formal requirements of the attainment of a certain level of skills confirmed by the diploma received, resulting in the importance of individuals' credential currency for the job market, were not abandoned. Thus, the underlying logic of the system (based on recognising and validating the level of merits as formal credentials) has been maintained.

What about socialisation?

In addition to the main systemic themes (grading, allocation, organisation of the pedagogical relationship), there is still an element of socialisation as one of the functions of schooling. Importantly, the situation of the pandemic and the experience of distance education drew attention to different aspects of school socialisation; in other words, a slightly divergent way of talking about the importance of social interaction in school. Before the pandemic, insofar as the discourse of school community or school relations appeared in the public debate, the focus was on the oppressive nature of school education. Moreover, pedagogical discourse strongly emphasised the dark side of the hidden curriculum of the school, defining it as "the prison of school". This rather derogatory rhetoric about schooling changed completely during the coronavirus outbreak, when, as we have already pointed out, it became clear that "going to school" has profound consequences for the personal development of young people. This contrasting, appreciative perception of school stems primarily from concerns about the increase in pupils' mental health issues and rising anxiety levels during school shutdowns, resulting from isolation and a lack of peer contact.

The second dimension of school institution turned out to be the childcaring role, which seemed to be unnoticed – or rather, taken for granted – until then. The pandemic revealed disruption in families' functioning due to the fact that children were learning from home. This situation limited adults' freedom (in some cases their ability) to go to work or work from home (especially for younger children's parents). It also disclosed the problem of the social division of labour, in which the school is responsible for arranging education, organising the pedagogical relationship and preparing children and young people for further stages of their biographies, not parents. Parents, who, especially in the asynchronous distance education model, had to step into the roles of educators and controllers of children's learning processes, realised and appreciated how significant the role of the teacher and the school is.

The situation of forced isolation accentuated the "ordinary patterns" of organising our daily activities and moving through the subsequent phases of biography within the framework of intra-generational mobility. During an "ordinary day", children attend school and parents go to work. Preparation for life in society takes place under the supervision of purposefully selected and trained personnel in places called schools. Children and adolescents assemble in these places where the individual characteristics of each pupil are formed.

There are no doubts that during the pandemic, education-based socialisation processes were also at work; however, the situation of distance education triggered other "packages of socialisation content" as part of the so-called hidden curriculum. Reports indicate that greater exposure to the acquisition of skills related to the use of digital technology comes to the fore here. In addition, the necessity of finding information on their own and the need to develop intrinsic motivation in achieving goals are often mentioned here. We have already discussed the issue of time management and work planning before. However, it is also worth remembering all the unintended consequences of being in a situation of isolation; the lack of physical co-presence of the teacher and other students. Such experiences create completely different habits regarding self-presentation, communication and body language. Being at school means being in a place where many micro-events happen, often simultaneously. In a virtual school setting, these events happen less often and with lesser intensity. In this model of schooling, pupils take part in a mediated relationship with an institution, a teacher and a group of other individuals who are also assigned to the same class.

The contrast between distance and in-person learning explains why, as soon as the crisis factor – the need for isolation – was withdrawn, we very quickly returned to our usual modus operandum. One could claim that the return to the traditional setting was accompanied by a certain social euphoria. Everyone was relieved that, finally, after months of being in a different mode of operation, things were back to normal. This overwhelming sense of relief was part of the experience of all school actors: students, teachers, principals, parents, as well as other professionals responsible for organising the education system. We have returned to "normalcy" because it provides us with safety and eliminates uncertainty associated with distance learning. We feel safe in that schooling that we know despite the fact that we complain about various aspects of the education system every day. It is important to realise that this is "normalcy" in the perspective of individual social actors (parents, teachers, students), but also from a systemic perspective. The situation of forced distance education has become not so much an opportunity to rethink school as we have learned to use new technologies in education, but rather an opportunity to see the fundamental principles of the system. In the absence of crisis, when things are how we expect them to be, we take reality for granted (including schooling with its educational solutions); however, in a situation with disruption to the system, we find it challenging to come up with alternative arrangements without disrupting the broader social order. An adequate analogy would be the idea that there is no need for military because (at the moment) there is no war. However, when war comes, it reveals the importance of the military system, its functions and purpose, as well as how it is related to other aspects of society's functioning. The situation is similar when it comes to education – the experience of the pandemic, which caused the dissemination of distance education, showed the importance of the ongoing and often unnoticed process occurring in school on a systemic and micro level.

It is vital to highlight that in the argument carried out in this book, technology does not appear very often as a factor of change. The hopes (and fears) for a change in school culture are associated with the technological saturation of modern reality. This desire for change stems from the original (axiomatic) assumption that the way schools work is inadequate to the logic of reality and even harmful to the development of individual freedom (the perspective of critical pedagogy). As a result, modern technologies should support the transformation of education by increasing students' independence, enabling them to learn in greater depth and in a more efficient way. The reason behind it is to master the skills we consider crucial in the modern world.

On the one hand, the discourse of technology in education does not negate the logic of the pedagogical relationship; on the other hand, it does not go beyond the discourse of modern rationality. Academics, headteachers, high-ranked decision-makers and other educational stakeholders from across the world are searching for better tools to develop the potential skills that we think (WE = those who make crucial decisions in and about education) are needed by modern citizens and employees. Thus, we are immersed in the logic of the system presented in our analytical model.

To reiterate, this logic implies a both-way direction of influence; on the one hand, the systemic needs of political, economic and individual nature which shape the mechanisms of the pedagogical relationship within the framework of the institution responsible for socialisation and allocation. On the other hand, the transformation of the latter elements will condition the operation of the social system and its expectations towards education. In summary, this is the core mechanism of social change of modern societies. Therefore, it can be argued that the tendency to maintain the model of school is conditioned by the constancy/persistence of systemic expectations. Technology in this regard changes nothing; it is only an element that potentially supports the implementation of roles and duties in a classically defined pedagogical relationship. As practice shows, digital technology is not taking hold in this classical model. It has somewhat become a tool to enable survival in times of crisis.

A way forward at the moment effectively means "business as usual" with traditional in-person schooling based on a clear division of time and space, where technology plays a minor role in the educational process and the pedagogical relationship revolves around the transmission of knowledge and assessment.

Following the "courageous imagination" approach by Khasnabish and Haiven, in the next chapter of the text, we will attempt to "imagine the world, life and social institutions not as they are, but as they might otherwise be" (Khasnabish et al., 2014: 3), thinking particularly about schooling.

Potential changes – Questions about institutional arrangements

It is clear that the operation of the school education system is deeply embedded in the logic of the functioning of the social system, as well as in the individual perceptions of its participants.

Is it possible, therefore, to change this logic?

Before tackling the above-raised question, it is useful to recall what directions of potential educational change have emerged during the coronavirus pandemic:

1 The vast majority of participants in the educational process have learned how to use digital technology to support their teaching and learning. Teachers and students have gained a new (potential) channel of communication in the implementation of the pedagogical relationship.
2 A physical space is not a *sine qua non* condition for schooling to take place. Thanks to technological advancements, we can imagine carrying out school tasks without gathering students in school buildings.

These two factors are the most tangible "inflection points" for potential educational change since their wider application will lead to the individualisation of educational processes. It is thanks to the change in regionalisation of schooling, in other words, the effect of stepping away from the school setting and shifting towards a home setting with the use of synchronous and asynchronous models of distance education (equivalent to the delivery of instruction). It became clear that the transformation of the place of teaching and learning (the *where*) – and of the timeframe of schooling (the *when*) – has an unquestionable impact on three pillars of traditional, in-person education: school roles – predominantly, the role of the teacher and the student (the pedagogical relationship), on ritualisation (school rules and routines, which recall and confirm the definition of the school situation, followed by the expected school behaviours), as well as on the hidden curriculum (unwritten rules of how to play the game of schooling successfully). In other words, the transformation of the *where* and the *when* significantly changes the *how* of schooling.

Most observers of educational processes see the potential for change precisely in this element. But at the same time, this discourse of change (i.e., of thinking about new forms of conducting education in a pedagogical relationship) does not negate the pedagogical relationship itself (the relationship between the learner and the teacher) nor negates the organisational consequences that result from this relationship – grading as a basic ritual and tool of control in this relationship. As a result, as could be observed during the pandemic, teachers and school institutions sought – at all costs – to fulfil the task of effectively fulfilling the role. In the definition of this role, full responsibility for the effectiveness of the educational process is enshrined (so far). In other words, it is the teacher and the educational institution that is treated as responsible for the learning outcomes of students. Despite decades of pedagogical discourse about increasing learner subjectivity and individualising education, it is those who teach that are seen as the ones to ensure the effectiveness of the process. Parents as well as educational authorities, representatives of the economy and, arguably, students to some extent blame the school system (the institution and its personnel) for the effects of the educational process. Importantly, teachers themselves think this, feeling guilty for the poor performance of students – this was evident in the frustration of educators during distance education when they did not feel they could fully control the educational process. It is also a sense of responsibility for the outcome that the need for control and power comes from. Assessment is, as we have already pointed out, both a way of verifying that the process went according to plan (whether the student learned what they needed to learn) and is, at the same time, a tool of control – a way of invoking such a definition of the situation in which teachers (school institution) are able to fulfil their commitment. As long as this commitment is on the side of the school institution with teachers as the personnel, it will not be possible to transform the logic of the pedagogical relationship. In this perspective, it is difficult to talk about a radical reconstruction of the general model of school work.

However, it cannot be assumed that absolutely nothing from the distance education experience will change teachers' repertoires and (consequently) students' roles. One can at least hope that there has been a taming of digital tools in education – students and teachers alike have seen that technology can be used successfully in learning processes. This means, at least for some teachers, an increase in the range of tools they can use in their work. It also increases, to some extent, the potential for students to seek knowledge on their own as a result and part of the education of digital competencies – the usefulness of which we saw during the pandemic (both in the education process itself and in professional and social life). It can be expected that there will be an even greater emphasis on the formation of digital skills as a task of the school.

The potential for change indicated here is, one might say, unimpressive. It does not significantly change the mechanisms that govern the educational process in the mass school system. If we wanted to significantly remodel the logic of the school's work, we would have to transform the key elements of this arrangement that we have indicated in our analytical model:

1 Transformation of the logic of the pedagogical relationship.
2 Moving away from grading.
3 Breaking with the model of a school tied to a physical presence in a certain place and time.

Transformation of the logic of the pedagogical relationship would have to consistently step away from the leading role of the teacher as the only one who signals opportunities and corrects mistakes. All responsibility for learning, in turn, would have to be on the students' shoulders. The ongoing debate about pupils' greater subjectivity and independence in their learning has been present in pedagogy for years. One can point to classic concepts of alternative education such as the Dalton Plan or the Montessori method. Continually, however, the figure of the teacher is assumed in this process, but they are the controller and (at the end of the day) are responsible for the outcomes in education. As we have already indicated, as long as we do not give up the teacher's responsibility for educational results, there will be no significant change in the pedagogical relationship. Making this change considerable would have to involve complete abandonment of grading as an element of the relationship. The only proxy for the effectiveness of education – the process of learning – would be the practical effectiveness of the subject's actions and their satisfaction. In other words, we would have to open up to an "on-demand" model of education in which the learner chooses what they need, at a time and in a form that suits them.

The lack of formal assessment at every educational threshold (primary, secondary, tertiary) would require thinking the unthinkable in the current times of modern "test-osis" (neologism from psychosis) where the tendency to put every aspect of pupils' learning to the test seems omnipresent (Woźniak, 2019). However, it is the way to reimagine and revolutionise the pedagogical relationship (the pedagogy), in which students – and students only – would have full ownership and control over their learning. Teachers, in turn, would only be the facilitators helping the pupils navigate their educational journey. Importantly, learners would have to be independent in personalising their curriculum and making decisions about their preferred subjects they choose to study in depth. They would also have to be internally motivated as, with the lack of assessment and grading, there would be no carrot-and-stick approach any longer.

The learning process itself would additionally be detached from the mechanisms of regionalisation and rituals hitherto associated with "going to school". Technological solutions already make it possible (as the pandemic experience has shown) for the learning process to take place wherever it is convenient for someone. Detached from the guidance of the physical space of the school (regionalisation), free from its compulsions, we would be able to focus on the learning content itself by seeking support from the teacher only when necessary. Technological developments (including artificial intelligence) may even cause us to seek and obtain this help from digital systems rather than live humans. As the experience of distance education at the time of the pandemic has already shown, some students found it more helpful to receive guidance on subject content from the internet than to receive the input from teachers (who, as all humans, can sometimes be boring or simply incompetent).

Potential consequences for the social functions of the school – Socialisation and allocation

Adopting such a model of the pedagogical relationship (Is it still a pedagogical relationship?) creates a whole broader consequence for the functioning of the school system, individuals and the social system as a whole. Abandoning grading and physical co-presence in the education process would have dramatic, transformative consequences for the social system. De facto, we are talking about the transformation of a huge segment of the culture and organisation of the social division of labour. We are talking directly about a society without school as a physical place inscribed in the landscape of the locality, without teachers, without the din of student shouts at recess, without daily meetings and rituals and without all the baggage of biographical experiences that (for the time being) each of us carries in the baggage of memories. To put it more formally, all of these have left a socialisation imprint on each of us.

The presented vision of the "new education system", with its own socialisation effects, a new set of communication skills, as well as interaction habits, is rather difficult to imagine at this point. It is a completely new model of society. With such a model of schooling, is it possible to preserve the implementation of the tasks that the social system sets before education? The proposed formula of the pedagogical relationship, in fact, education outside of it, does not provide a resolution to the two key tasks of the education system – socialisation into the socio-political community and the handling of selection and allocation processes in the occupational structure and in the system of social stratification.

The socialisation function of the school is a non-trivial question. As we pointed out in Chapter 2, the formation of individuals as subjects of social action is the task of the mass education system, which, in modern society, complements the action of the family and community. The school, the system of mass education, is a tool for colonising particularistic life worlds by the logic of the system, the state, the nation, etc. (Habermas, 1984). It is through the medium of school and the entire set of rituals and mechanisms of the school's overt and covert programme that social cohesion is ensured at the level of the local community and the nation-state as a whole. With the consequent individualisation of learning processes and the disappearance of the pedagogical relationship (and with the disappearance of rituals in the physical place of the school), the system will require another medium for colonising mass consciousness. It is difficult to adjudicate what this will be. On the one hand, we can expect a retreat towards the commons. While modernisation was a process of moving away from the Gemeinschaft model towards Gesselschaft (to use the language of F. Toenies), the disappearance of the institution of the school as we know it could mean a return to the importance of socialisation processes in the local community, neighbourhood and family. At the other extreme, here is the potential for hyper-individualisation based on socialisation in a virtual network society (Castells, 2000). This is a message shaped in spontaneous, systemically unmodelled, dependent-on-the-individual communication experiences of participants in network interactions.

Somewhat marginal, in this context, may seem to be the question of child and youth care. However, it is a very important question concerning the social organisation of individuals' time. What can we do with this mass of children and teenagers? In pre-industrial times, this was not an issue as children were very quickly integrated into economic processes. Today, however, childhood functions as a specific time of exclusion from professional obligations. The same applies to the category of youth, which is a time of specific social moratorium (Erikson). As the experience of the pandemic has shown, it is these functions of providing care for children when parents work that may remain the sole function of the school institution in the classical sense of gathering individuals in a specific place.

The second, equally important task of education is the formation of trajectories of placement of individuals in the social structure through paths of acquiring a profession. The problem of the allocative function of school are de facto two parallel problem fields: on the one hand, the task of estimating the substantive suitability of individuals to perform specific tasks in the system of the social division of labour; on the other hand, it is a question of preserving the principle of equality of opportunity, which means questions about social inequalities in access to the best professional positions. This is because it is necessary here to remember the differentiated social rewards (money, power, prestige) associated with certain positions in the social system. The field of education is a field of selection and struggle for access to the best positions. It is in this tension between meritocracy and the discourse of equal opportunity that the constant process of clashing economic tasks with the satisfaction of the individual needs of citizens is evident (as we pointed out in Chapter 2).

When grades are abandoned as an element of the pedagogical relationship, questions arise about the logic of filling social positions while maintaining the principles of meritocracy. In this scenario, the selective and allocative function of the education system would fade; therefore, it would only be the workplaces that would verify young adults' employability in terms of their skills and knowledge to meet their standards (the question is how they would go about it, whether they would require their potential employees to take a test beforehand, or whether they would judge the employees' suitability by their performance at work).

In effect, another vital question arises as to whether this unconventional and unconfining way of education (Reay, 2020) would minimise or rather exacerbate educational inequalities even further? Would the lack of exams enhance or hinder pupils' determination and curiosity towards learning? Bourdieu, amongst many structuralists, provides us with a clear answer – most likely, pupils from families of high cultural capital and high employment status would have a much easier task in terms of their self-motivation and self-discipline to learn (as well as their appreciation of education) as opposed to pupils from low-income families whose limited cultural and economic capital does not provide them with an incentive to learn. Therefore, parents with a low socio-economic status would likely be more willing to encourage their children to acquire practical skills that would enable them to earn their wages as soon as possible. This is not because they do not value education in itself; we know they do (Lareau, 2003). It is rather because of their circumstances, which determine differences to high-status parents' attitudes towards schooling and, thus, result in their children's lower level of motivation to learn.

On the one hand, the proposed idea of the education system appears to be free from oppression and symbolic violence (Bourdieu, 1984) due to the transformation of pedagogical relationship and the hidden curriculum; on the other hand, however, there is an issue of potential lack of pupils' intrinsic motivation, necessary to succeed in the new educational environment, as well as digital inequalities, such as unequal access to distance education because of the limited access to software, hardware and technological skills (Reay, 2020). The latter, commonly known as the digital divide, would be rather staggering as it appears to be one of the main obstacles in the way to revolutionising education, often omitted or discussed very briefly by the enthusiasts of change, who – apart from acknowledging the issue – unfortunately do not suggest any tangible solutions of how to "wipe it out" (Zhao, Watterston, 2021: 10).

A slightly different scenario could potentially involve the lack of day-to-day assessment and grading; however, at the end of each educational stage, there would be a formal exam (confirming the acquisition of the knowledge and skills [by the learners]) allowing them to move on to the next educational phase. However, the issue of the digital divide and motivation still stands in this case.

As can be seen, the redefinition of the logic of the pedagogical relationship can have very far-reaching effects on the processes of levelling social inequality through education. In fact, the democratising function of formal education, which in its current form at least gives all citizens a chance to participate in the race for social merits on relatively similar terms, may be undermined. There is a risk here of intensifying the processes of re-feudalisation by education (Beck) (i.e., a return to the even unequivocal importance of origin status in the processes of social mobility).

Conclusion

Chapter 2 offers an interpretation of the experience of distance education during the COVID-19 crisis. The analytical model, proposed in Chapter 2, enables the reader to understand the reaction of the main school actors (principals, teachers, students and parents) to the experience of distance education. Their sense of relief, when it comes to returning to the "normal" operation of schools, becomes understandable. Forced isolation and distance education imposed an unprecedented pressure on the key elements of the education system and consequently, they created a struggle to maintain the rules of the pedagogical relationship. At the same time, it was a struggle to preserve the implementation of the main functions of the school – socialisation and allocation.

The experience of distance education, with the widespread use of digital devices, did not result in universal, in-depth reflection on the logic of the pedagogical relationship and, thus, did not become the basis for "rethinking school". In our analyses, we have tried to show several dimensions of the systemic challenges associated with transforming the pedagogical relationship and moving away from mass schooling defined by the physical space of school. The questions that occur at this point require further debate. A profound reconstruction of the way education is organised seems challenging, if not impossible, under the operating conditions of the systemic logic of modernity. If such changes were to occur, they would involve a transformation of the social system. Perhaps the society of late modernity is slowly maturing for this historical transformation, similar in effect, to the transition from traditional to modern society. This is what Ulrich Beck (2016), for example, implies by discussing the accelerated development of science and technology, which could potentially contribute to the transformation of the principles of the organisation of social life.

Ending: What comes next?

The purpose of this book was to propose a comprehensive model of analysis for the processes which emerged during the experience of distance education at the time of the COVID-19 pandemic. The starting point was an observation that despite the severe perturbations during the pandemic and the implementation of several organisational changes – such as the unprecedented in its scale use of digital technologies as a result of the crisis – a significant change in the logic of schooling did not occur. Schooling's extraordinary resistance to change, observed amongst the education systems worldwide, has been explained and interpreted thanks to the proposed analytical model presented in this volume.

We began our deliberations by analysing the cases of two education systems (Poland and the UK) facing the COVID-19 crisis. This comparative analysis enabled us to identify the differences in both countries' responses; however, it also allowed us to distinguish the universal problems that occurred, regardless of the unique circumstances that both nations – with their different education systems – had found themselves in. Operating in the distance education model as a result of the pandemic, education systems struggled with the socialisation of future generations and the allocation of individuals in the social structure. These reflections became a vital step towards reconstructing the key principles of schooling in modern societies, as presented in Chapter 2. The proposed analytical model defines the school culture as a result of the organisation of the school institution, underpinned by the logic of the pedagogical relationship. At the same time, every school is the basic organisational unit of schooling, which responds to the needs of the social system. However, the latter – according to the logic of modernity – is a system where the needs of the nation-state, the economy and the individual subjects, clash. Therefore, it is essential to reiterate the ten principles for the functioning of the social system:

1. the implementation of the task of preparing citizens, workers and self-determined individuals takes place in the system of the institutionalised process of training in places called schools;
2. in these places, the formation of specific structures for defining the tasks of participants in this world takes place based on the logic of the pedagogical relationship;
3. the implementation of this relationship is subject to considerations arising from the nature of the pedagogical relationship itself as well as from systemic expectations;
4. these systemic expectations are to secure the realisation of the unstable balance between the needs of the state, the economy and individual units (families);
5. the persistence of the determinants underpinning the pedagogical relationship at school is ensured by the mechanisms of regionalisation and routinisation (ritualisation).
6. assessment and grading are the natural consequence of the implementation of the pedagogical relationship as the basic control disposition of the effects of its implementation;
7. grading is both a function of the pedagogical relationship and the fulfilment of the requirements of the system – politically, economically and individually;
8. the task of the education system is to organise the structures and tools of assessment;
9. grading (assessment) becomes a basic control ritual and sets the tone for patterns of interaction in school – it is subject to routinisation;
10. the importance of physical co-presence and the hidden curriculum of the school – all processes of shaping pedagogical relations in terms of serving the systemic needs of the society happens in the physical settings of school settlement.

The comprehensive model of schooling in modern societies laid out in this book provides an interpretation of the experience of the COVID-19 phenomenon and its meaning for education system. It elucidates why we did not observe a profound change in the school culture after the pandemic subsided. At the same time, it allows us to derive hypotheses about the future and the possible consequences of adopting solutions emerging as potential avenues for educational change.

The futuristic vision presented in Chapter 3 – of a thorough transformation of the school system and the consequent transformation of the social system – is radical and yet probably utopian. The systemic logic of modern societies produces such an overwhelming range of influences on the solutions of the education system that it is very difficult to imagine radical transformations of the pedagogical attitude. The most likely scenario is the partial adaptation of technological solutions that teachers may have learned (on a large scale) during the forced distance education at the time of the pandemic. Undoubtedly, the most recommended way forward so far is the so-called "balanced approach", envisaging schooling as the combination of in-person and distance education in the form of blended learning. Its enthusiasts claim that "it is vital to combine the power of technology and the power of communities" (The World Economic Forum, 2022). Others, in turn, argue that, apart from the very learning, the sense of community defined by the need to belong and share is at the essence of the educational process, which can only be fulfilled in the traditional face-to-face form with some elements of distance learning (Rovai, 2002).

The complexity of the process of rethinking our (universal at its core) education system is profound. The educational experiment that happened during the pandemic should not necessarily be used to legitimise strong statements about the inevitable change of schooling – which, according to some scholars, has already happened (Castells, 2020) or "will happen, we just do not know how it will look like" (Fullan, 2020: 25). Following the thought of Diane Reay, who argues that the real transformation requires the "revolution in national psyche" (Reay, 2020: 320), we should instead reflect on what school(ing) is and what its main functions are in relation to three key spheres: the state, the economy and the individuals in order to talk about potential change.

In light of the current, post-COVID academic debate about digitalisation and the future of schooling, the general pandemic experiences of education systems worldwide were similar. They indicated that distance education was a survival strategy and an emergency option, not a long-term alternative and a chance for schooling to be revolutionised. This very context brings an analogy to what Winston Churchill said about democracy in November 1947. What it feels like could be said about in-person schooling: "Indeed it has been said that democracy is the worst form of government except for all those other forms that have been tried from time to time" (International Churchill Society, 2016). Perhaps the schooling we know, in its traditional face-to-face form, is the worst form of teaching and learning, except for other forms (such as hybrid and blended, or synchronous and asynchronous distance education models) that have been tried from time to time?

In our analyses, we have attempted to show an analytical model that makes possible to synthesise the experience of distance education as experienced by all educational systems in the world. At the same time, this very model provides the reader with an explanation of why the historical experience of COVID-19 has had such a minor impact on the functioning of education systems. The basic mechanisms of the mass education system in modern societies are key to understand the mechanisms of change in education. Significantly, it is crucial to realise the dialectical arrangement of the functioning of educational institutions as subordinated to the implementation of the vital systemic tasks of preserving the cohesion of the socio-political system, providing human resources for the economy and creating conditions for the socialisation of individuals as subjects of social action. This arrangement of systemic expectations underlies the organisation of the institution, which – in turn – operates in the micro-world of school events based on the logic of the pedagogical relationship.

It is not that school education has not changed since its inception and dissemination at the turn of the 20th century. School culture, the rules of relationships between teachers and students and the repertoire of behaviours they have at their disposal in playing their roles are significantly different today from that of the early 20th century. What remains unchanged, however, is the logic of the relationship between the teacher and the learner – the supreme importance of assessment. This very "packaging" of the pedagogical relationship, in the form of a repertoire of behaviours of school drama actors, changes following variations in the logic of the social system of which the school system is a part and for which it works. As the importance of individual freedom and subjectivity increases, the margin of freedom in conduct increases, and the extent of the teacher's power over pupils' behaviour decreases. To reiterate, however, the core principle which organises school order – the logic of the pedagogical relationship – does not change. It is this conundrum that might be one of the most important sociological findings about education that we have come to through the analyses of the COVID-19 pandemic experience.

Bibliography

Anderson Jenny, 2020, 'World vs Coronavirus', Quartz (Retrieved from: https://qz.com/1826369/how-coronavirus-is-changing-education/).
Apple Michael, 1982, *Education and Power*, London: Routledge and Kegan Paul.
Apple Michael, 2004, *Ideology and Curriculum Third Edition*, London: Routledge and Kegan Paul.
Baker David P., 2009a, 'The Educational Transformation of Work: Towards a New Synthesis', Journal of Education and Work, Vol. 22, No. 3, pp. 163–191.
Baker David P., 2009b, *The Schooled Society. The Educational Transformation of Global Culture*, Stanford: Stanford University Press.
Baker David P., 2011, The future of schooled society: The transforming culture of education in postindustrial society in: Maureen Hallinan (ed.), *Frontiers in Sociology of Education*, Dordrecht: Springer, pp. 11–34.
Ball Stephen J., 1993, 'Education Markets, Choice and Social Class: The Market as a Class Strategy in the UK and the USA', British Journal of Sociology of Education, Vol. 14, No. 1, pp. 3–19.
Ball Stephen, 2003, *Class Strategies and the Educational Market. The Middle Classes and Social Advantage*, London: Routledge Falmer.
Baxter Hugh, 1987, 'System and Life-World in Habermas's "Theory of Communicative Action"', Theory and Society, Vol. 16, No. 1, pp. 39–86.
Beauchamp Gary, Hulme Moira, Clarke Linda, Hamilton Lorna, Harvey Janet A., 2021, 'People Miss People: A Study of School Leadership and Management in the Four Nations of the United Kingdom in the Early Stage of the COVID-19 Pandemic', Educational Management Administration & Leadership, Vol. 49, No. 3, pp. 375–392.
Beck Urlich, 2016, *The Metamorphosis of the World: How Climate Change Is Transforming Our Concept of the World*, United Kingdom: Polity Press.
Becker Gary S., 1964, *Human Capital: A Theoretical and Empirical Analysis, with Special Reference to Education*, Chicago: University of Chicago Press.
Berger Peter L., Luckmann Thomas, 2010, *Społeczne tworzenie rzeczywistości*, Traktat z socjologii, Warszawa: wiedzy, Polskie Wydawnictwo Naukowe PWN.

Bibliography

Blau Peter M., Duncan Otis D., 1967, *American Occupational Structure*, New York: Macmillan.

Boli John, Ramirez Francisco O., Meyer John W.,1985, 'Explaining the Origins and Expansion of Mass Education', Comparative Education Review, Vol. 29, No. 2, pp. 145–170

Borio Claudio, 2020, 'The Covid-19 Economic Crisis: Dangerously Unique', Business Economics, Vol. 55, pp. 181–190.

Boudon Raymond, 1982, *The Unintended Consequences of Social Action*, London: St. Martin's Press.

Boudon Raymond, 2008, *Efekt odwrócenia. Niezamierzone skutki działań społecznych*, translated by Agnieszka Karpowicz, Warszawa: Oficyna Naukowa

Bourdieu Pierre, 1984, *Distinction. A Social Critique of the Judgement of Taste*, Cambridge, MA: Harvard University Press.

Bourdieu Pierre, Passeron Jean-Claude, 2011, *Reprodukcja. Elementy teorii systemu nauczania*, transl. Elżbieta Neyman, Warszawa: Wydawnictwo Naukowe PWN.

Bowles Samuel, Gintis Herbert, 2002, 'Schooling in Capitalist America Revisited', Sociology of Education, Vol. 75, No. 1, pp. 1–18.

Bowles Samuel, Gintis Herbert, 2011, *Schooling in Capitalist America*, New York: Basic Books.

Buchner Anna, Biernat Magdalena, Majchrzak Marta, Maria Wierzbicka, edycja I, Raport z badań, 2020, 'Edukacja zdalna w czasie pandemii' (Retrieved from: https://centrumcyfrowe.pl/wp-content/uploads/sites/16/2020/05/Edukacja_zdalna_w_czasie_pandemii.pptx-2.pdf).

Buchner Anna, Wierzbicka Maria, Raport z badań, 2020, ed II, 'Edukacja zdalna w czasie pandemii' (Retrieved from: https://centrumcyfrowe.pl/wp-content/uploads/sites/16/2020/11/Raport_Edukacja-zdalna-w-czasie-pandemii.-Edycja-II.pdf).

Całek Grzegorz, 2021, Raport: Jak się zmieniła edukacja zdalna w czasie pandemii COVID-19?, UW Centrum Współpracy i Dialogu.

Cambridge Assessment, 2020a, Covid-19 Curriculum Watch: Education Policy in the First 3 Months of the Pandemic, (Retrieved from: https://www.cambridgeassessment.org.uk/insights/uk-education-policy-during-Covid-19-pandemic-topic-one/).

Cambridge Assessment, 2020b, Covid-19 Curriculum Watch 2: Changes to Assessment in Response to the Pandemic, (Retrieved from: https://www.cambridgeassessment.org.uk/insights/uk-changes-to-assessment-during-Covid-19-pandemic-topic-two/).

Cambridge Assessment, 2020c, Covid-19 Curriculum Watch 3: Learning Access, Resources, and Assessment Guidance during the Pandemic, (Retrieved from: https://www.cambridgeassessment.org.uk/insights/learning-access-resources-and-assessment-guidance-during-Covid-19-pandemic-topic-three/).

Cambridge Assessment, 2020d, 'Covid-19 Curriculum Watch 4: Curriculum Choices and the Pandemic', (Retrieved from: https://www.cambridgeassessment.org.uk/insights/curriculum-choices-and-the-pandemic-curriculum-watch-topic-four/).

Cambridge Report, 2020, 'Shock to the System', Part 2, Cambridge Educate.
Cambridge Report, 2021, 'What Have We Learned about the COVID-19 Impact on Education so Far?' Transforming Societies Through Education.
Castells Manuel, 2000, *The Rise of the Network Society*, 2nd ed., Vol. I, Malden, USA: Blackwell Publishing.
Castells Manuel, 2020, 'Castells Debate Pandemia', Publico e Educacao. Outras Palavras, (Retrieved from: https://outraspalavras.net/poscapitalismo/castells-debate-a-pandemia-o-publico-e-a-educacao/).
Coleman Victoria, 2021, 'Digital Divide in UK Education during the COVID-19 Pandemic: Literature Review', Cambridge Assessment.
Collins Randall, 1979, *The Credential Society*, New York: Academic Press.
Collins Randall, 2000, Comparative and historical patterns of education in: Maureen T. Hallinan (ed.), *Handbook of the Sociology of Education*, New York: Kluwer Academic/Plenum Publishers, pp. 213–240.
Crawford Joseph, Butler-Henderson Kerryn, Rudolph Jürgen, Glowatz Matt, Burton Rob, Malkawi Bashar, Magni Paola A., Lam Sophia, 2020, 'COVID-19: 20 Countries' Higher Education Intra-Period Digital Pedagogy Responses', Journal of Applied Learning & Teaching, Vol. 3, No. 1, pp. 9–28.
Cullinane Carl, Montacute Rebecca, 2020, 'COVID-19 and Social Mobility Impact Brief #1: School Shutdown', Research Brief, pp. 1–11.
Da Silva Vieira, Marili Moreira, Barbosa Susana Mesquita, 2020, 'School Culture and Innovation: Does the Post-Pandemic World COVID-19 Invite to Transition or to Rupture?', European Journal of Social Science, Education and Research, Vol. 7, No. 2, pp. 23–34.
Darby Flower, 2020, '5 Low-Tech, Time-Saving Ways to Teach Online during Covid-19', Chronicle of Higher Education (Retrieved from: https://www.chronicle.com/article/5-Low-Tech-Time-Saving-Ways/248519).
Davies Scott, Guppy Neil, 2010, *The Schooled Society. An Introduction to the Sociology of Education*, Don Mills: Oxford University Press.
Davis Kingsley, 1966, *Human Society*, New York: The Macmillan.
Dehler Gordon E., Welsh Ann M., 2014, 'Against Spoon-Feeding. For Learning. Reflections on Students' Claims to Knowledge', Journal of Management Education 2014, Vol. 38, No. 6, pp. 875–893.
Department for Education, 2021, 'Guidance: Schools Coronavirus (COVID-19) Operational Guidance', (Retrieved from: https://www.gov.uk/government/publications/actions-for-schools-during-thecoronavirus-outbreak/schools-coronavirus-covid-19-operational-guidance).
Długosz Piotr, 2022, 'Kondycja psychiczna uczniów zamieszkałych na peryferiach po trzech miesiącach od powrotu do szkoły', Youth in Central and Eastern Europe, Vol. 9, No. 13, pp. 1–7.
Dorn Emma, Hancock Bryan, Sarakatsannis Jimmy, Viruleg Ellen, 2020, 'COVID-19 and Student Learning in the United States: The Hurt Could Last a Lifetime', McKinsey, (Retrieved from: https://www.mckinsey.com/industries/public-and-social-sector/our-insights/covid-19-and-student-learning-in-the-united-states-the-hurt-could-last-a-lifetime).

Draus Jan, Terlecki Ryszard, 2006, Historia wychowania. *Wiek XIX i XX*, Kraków: WAM.

Dreeben Robert, 1968, *On What Is Learned in School*, Reading: Addison-Wesley.

Duncan Otis D., Blau Peter, 1967, *The American Occupational Structure*, New York: Wiley.

Dupriez Vincent, Dumay Xavier, 2006, 'Inequalities in School Systems: Effect of School Structure or of Society Structure?', Comparative Education, Vol. 42, No. 2, pp. 243–260.

Durkheim Émile, 1956, Education: Its nature and its role in: Émile Blau (ed.), *Education and Sociology*, trans. Sherwood D. Fox, Glencoe: The Free Press, pp. 61–90.

Duru-Bellat Marie, 2009, Educational expansion and the evolution of inequalities of opportunity in France in: Andreas Hadjar, Rolf Becker (eds.), *Expected and Unexpected Consequences of the Educational Expansion in Europe and the US: Theoretical Approaches and Empirical Findings in Comparative Perspective*, Bern: Haupt, pp. 49–56.

Education Policy Institute, 2021, 'EPI Research for the Department for Education on Pupil Learning Loss', (Retrieved from: https://epi.org.uk/publications-and-research/epi-research-for-the-department-for-education-on-pupil-learning-loss/).

Feinberg Walter, Soltis Jonas F., 2000, *Szkoła i społeczeństwo*, tłum. Krzysztof Kruszewicz, Warszawa: Wydawnictwa Szkolne i Pedagogiczne.

Ferdig Richard E., Kennedy Kathryn, 2014, *Handbook of Research on K-12 Online and Blended Learning*, ETC Press, p.180.

Ferguson Donna, Savage Michael, 2020, 'We're Still Waiting: Poorer GCSE Pupils Left without Laptops Despite Government Pledge', Observer, (Retrieved from: https://www.theguardian.com/education/2020/jun/07/were-still-waiting-schools-still-lack-free-laptops-pledged-to-help-poorer-gcse-pupils).

Fleming Ted, 2002, Habermas on Civil Society, Lifeworld and System: Unearthing the Social in Transformation Theory, Teachers College Record, 2002, pp. 1–17.

Fleming Ted (2002). Habermas on civil society, lifeworld and system: Unearthing the social in Transformation Theory, Teachers College Record, 2002, 1–17, https://www.tcrecord.org/content.asp?ContentID=10877

Floud Jean, Halsey Albert H., 1959, 'Education and Social Structure: Theories and Methods', Harvard Educational Review, Vol. 29, No. 4, pp. 288–296.

Fotheringham Peter, Harriott Thomas, Healy Grace, Arenge Gabby, McGill Ross, Wilson Elaine, 2020, 'Pressures and Influences on School Leaders as Policy Makers during COVID-19'. Cambridge, UCL, (Retrieved from: https://papers.ssrn.com/sol3/papers.cfm?abstract_id=3642919).

Frey Carl Benedikt, 2020, 'Technology at Work v5.0. The New Normal of Remote Work', Citi GPS: Global Perspectives & Solutions, (Retrieved from: https://www.citivelocity.com/citigps/technology-at-work-v5-0/).

Fullan Michael, 2020, 'Learning and the Pandemic: What's Next?', Prospects, Vol. 49, pp. 25–28.

'GCSE, AS and A level: Autumn and November 2020 exam series', 2020, (Retrieved from: https://www.gov.uk/government/publications/gcse-as-and-a-level-autumn-and-november-2020-exam-series).

Gdula Maciej, Sadura Piotr, 2012, *Style życia i porządek klasowy w Polsce*, Scholar.

Giddens Anthony, 1984, *The Constitution of Society*, CA, USA: University of California Press.

'GL Assessment', 2021, (Retrieved from: https://www.gl-assessment.co.uk/).

Głos Nauczycielski, 2022, 'Ile dzieci i młodzieży z Ukrainy będzie się uczyć w polskich szkołach od września? Czarnek podał nową liczbę', (Retrieved from: https://glos.pl/ilu-uczniow-z-ukrainy-bedzie-sie-uczyc-w-polskich-szkolach-od-wrzesnia-czarnek-podal-nowa-liczbe).

Goffman Erving, 1990, *The Presentation of Self in Everyday Life*, Reprint ed., Penguin.

Gonzalez-Nieto Noé Abraham, Garcia-Hernandez Caridad, Espinosa-Meneses Margarita, 2021, 'School Culture and Digital Technologies: Educational Practices at Universities within the Context of the COVID-19 Pandemic', Future Internet, Vol. 13, No. 246, pp. 1–22.

Gozgor Giray, 2022, 'Global Evidence on the Determinants of Public Trust in Governments during the COVID-19', Applied Research in Quality of Life, Vol. 17, pp. 559–578.

Green Andy, 1991, *Education and State Formation: The Rise of Education Systems in England, France, and the USA*, London: Palgrave Macmillan.

Gromkowska-Melosik Agnieszka, 2017, *Testy edukacyjne. Studium dynamiki selekcji i socjalizacji*, Poznań: UAM.

Gustiani Sri, 2020, 'Students' Motivation in Online Learning during the COVID-19 Pandemic Era: A Case Study', Holistics Journal, Vol. 12, No. 2, pp. 23–40.

Habermas Jurgen, 1984, Theory of communicative action Vol. 1, *Reason and the Rationalisation of Society*, Boston: Beacon Press.

Hadjar Andreas, Becker Rolf, 2009, Educational expansion: Expected and unexpected consequences in: Andreas Hadjar, Rolf Becker (eds.), *Expected and Unexpected Consequences of the Educational Expansion in Europe and the US: Theoretical Approaches and Empirical Findings in Comparative Perspective*, Bern: Haupt, pp. 9–26.

Haller Archibald, Portes Alejandro, 2011, Status attainment processes in: Richard Arum, Irenee R. Beattie, Karly Ford (eds.), *The Structure of Schooling. Readings in Sociology of Education*, Los Angeles: Sage, pp. 23–30.

Head David, 1974, *Free Way to Learning*, Harmondsworth: Penguin Education Hogan David, 1996, 'To Better Our Condition: Educational Credentialing and 'the Silent Compulsion of Economic Relations' in the United States, 1830 to the Present', History of Education Quarterly, Vol. 36, pp. 243–270.

Holmes Richard, 2020, 'Evidence Is Clear: Teachers Are Doing All They Can', (Retrieved from: https://www.tes.com/magazine/archive/evidence-clear-teachers-are-doing-all-they-can).

Igielska Beata, 2020, 'W kryzysowej sytuacji szkoły oczekują jasnych przepisów i wytycznych', (Retrieved from: https://www.prawo.pl/oswiata/funkcjonowanie-szkoly-w-czasie-epidemii-koronawirusa-wywiad-z,500138.html).

'Ile dzieci i młodzieży z Ukrainy będzie się uczyć w polskich szkołach od września?', 2022, Głos nauczycielski, (Retrieved from: https://glos.pl/iluuczniow-z-ukrainy-bedzie-sie-uczyc-w-polskich-szkolach-od-wrzesnia-czarnek-podal-nowa-liczbe).

International Churchill Society, 2016, 'The Worst Form of Government', (Retrieved from: https://winstonchurchill.org/resources/quotes/the-worst-form-of-government/).

Jackson Phillip W., 1968, *Life in Classroom*, New York: Holt, Reinhart and Winston.

Janowski Andrzej, 1995, *Uczeń w teatrze życia szkolnego*, Warszawa: WSiP.

Karabel Jerome, Halsey Albert. H., (eds.), 1977, *Power and Ideology in Education*, New York: Oxford University Press.

Keedie Nell, 1971, Knowledge and control: New directions for the sociology of education in: Michael Young (ed.), *Classroom Knowledge*, London: Collier-Macmillan, pp. 133–160.

Kerckhoff Alan C., 1995, 'Institutional Arrangements and Stratification Processes Un Industrial Societies', Annual Review of Sociology, Vol. 21, pp. 323–347.

Khasnabish Alex, Haiven Max, 2014, *The Radical Imagination: Social Movement Research in the Age of Austerity*, London: Bloomsbury.

Kim Lisa E., Leary Rowena, Asbury Kathryn, 2021, 'Teachers' Narratives during COVID-19 Partial School Reopenings: An Exploratory study', Educational Research; a Review for Teachers and All Concerned with Progress in Education, Vol. 63, No. 2, pp. 244–260.

Kolanowska Ewa, 2020, *The System of Education in Poland*, Eurydice: FRSE Publications.

Kwieciński Zbigniew, 1995, *Dynamika funkcjonowania szkoły*, Studium empiryczne z socjologii.

Kwieciński Zbigniew, 2002, *Wykluczanie*, Toruń: Wydawnictwo Naukowe UMK.

Labaree David F., 2012, *Someone Has to Fail. The Zero-Sum Game of Public Schooling*, Cambridge, MA, and London, England: Harvard University Press.

Lareau Anette, 2003, *Unequal Childhoods Unequal Childhoods: Class, Race, and Family Life*, CA, USA: University of California Press.

Litak Stanisław, 2005, *Historia wychowania. Do Wielkiej Rewolucji Francuskiej*, Kraków: WAM

Lough Catherine, 2020, 'Coronavirus: Eton Offers Free Courses to State Pupils', TES, (Retrieved from: https://www.tes.com/magazine/archive/coronavirus-eton-offers-free-courses-state-pupils).

Lucas Megan, Nelson Julie, Sims David, 2020, Schools' Responses to Covid-19: Pupil Engagement in Remote Learning. National foundation for Educational Research [NFER], (Retrieved from: https://www.nfer.ac.uk/media/4073/schools_responses_to_covid_19_pupil_engagement_in_remote_learning.pdf).

Lucas Samuel R., 2001, 'Effectively Maintained Inequality: Education Transitions, Track Mobility, and Social Background Effects', The American Journal of Sociology, Vol. 106, No. 6, pp. 1642–1690.

Luckin Rose, 2017, 'Towards Artificial Intelligence-Based Assessment Systems', Nature Human Behaviour, Vol. 1, No. 3, p. 0028, (Retrieved from: https://www.nature.com/articles/s41562-016-0028).

Lynch Kathleen, 1989, *The Hidden Curriculum: Reproduction in Education, a Reappraisal*, London and New York: The Falmer Press.

Manyukhina Yana, Hamlyn Helen, 2021, 'Living and Learning during a Pandemic: The Views and Experiences of Primary School Children', UCL (Retrieved from: https://discovery.ucl.ac.uk/id/eprint/10128318/1/Manyukhina_Living_and_Learning_Pandemic.pdf)

McLaren Peter, 1986, *Schooling as a Ritual Performance*, London: Routledge and Kegan Paul.

McLaren Peter, 1989, *Life in Schools: An Introduction to Critical Pedagogy in the Foundations of Education*, New York and London: Longman.

Meighan Roland, 1993, *Socjologia edukacji*, tłum. Ewa Kiszkurno-Koziej, Zofia Knutsen, Piotr Kwieciński, Toruń: UMK.

Meyer John, 2011, The effects of education as an institution in: Richard Arum, Irenee R. Beattie, Karly Ford (eds.), *The Structure of Schooling. Readings in Sociology of Education*, Los Angeles: Sage, pp. 510–519.

Mikiewicz Piotr, 2005, *Społeczne światy szkół średnich. Trajektorie marginesu i trajektorie elit*, Wrocław: DSW.

Mikiewicz Piotr, 2016, *Socjologia edukacji. Teorie, koncepcje, pojęcia*, Warszawa: PWN.

Mikiewicz Piotr, 2017, 'Oblicza socjologii edukacji – w stronę syntetycznego modelu analiz', Edukacja, Vol. 3, No. 142, pp. 5–19.

Mikiewicz Piotr, 2020, 'Educationalisation and its implications for contemporary society', Dyskursy Młodych Andragogów/Adult Education Discourses', No. 21, 9–19.

Mikiewicz Piotr, Jurczak-Morris Marta, Barzak Justyna, 2022, 'Wyłaniająca się nowa kultura szkoły wraz z jej potencjalnymi konsekwencjami w kontekście edukacji zdalnej w czasie pandemii COVID-19?', Youth in Central and Eastern Europe, Vol. 9, No. 13, pp. 1–6.

Ministerstwo Edukacji i Nauki, 2020, 'Matura 2020 – wyniki egzaminu w sesji głównej' (Retrieved from: https://www.gov.pl/web/edukacja-i-nauka/matura-2020-wyniki-egzaminu-w-sesji-glownej#:~:text=Egzamin%20maturalny%20ze%20wszystkich%20przedmiot%C3%B3w,z%20j%C4%99zyka%20angielskiego%2092%20proc).

Moore Rob, 2008, *Education and Society. Issues and Explanations in the Sociology of Education*, Cambridge: Polity Press.

Myck Michał, Oczkowska Monika, Trzciński Kajetan, 2020, 'Zamknięte szkoły: warunki uczniów do nauki zdalnej w okresie pandemii COVID-19', (Retrieved from: https://cenea.org.pl/wp-content/uploads/2020/03/komentarz_20200328.pdf).

Nowotniak Justyna, 2011, 'Społeczne światy pokoi nauczycielskich', Człowiek, Teraźniejszość, Edukacja, Nr, Vol. 3, No. 55, pp. 71–86.

Nyhan Barry, 2002, Knowledge development, research and collaborative learning in: Barry Nyhan (ed.), *Taking Steps towards the Knowledge Society: Reflections on the Process of Knowledge Development*, Luxemburg: Office for Official Publications of the European Communities, pp. 18–38.

OECD, 2020a, Education and COVID-19: Focusing on the Long-Term Impact of School Closures In: Tackling CORONAVIRUS(COVID-19): Contributing to a Global Effort.

OECD, 2020b, Education Responses to COVID-19: An Implementation Strategy Toolkit in: Education Policy Perspectives.

OECD, 2020c, A Framework to Guide an Education Response to the COVID-19 Pandemic of 2020.

OECD, 2021, The State of Global Education. 18 Months into the Pandemic.

OECD, 2022, First Lessons from Government Evaluations of COVID-19 Responses: A Synthesis.

Olugboji Olufunnke Abidemi, 2022, *Teacher-Pupil Interaction and Distance Learning in Emergency Periods: The England and Wales Experience*, University of East Anglia, pp. 1–18.

Pallas Aaron M., 2000, The effect of schooling on individual lives, w: Maureen T. Hallinan (ed.), *Handbook of the Sociology of Education*, New York: Kluwer Academic/Plenum.

Parsons Talcott, 1959, 'The School Class as a Social System', Harvard Educational Review, Vol. 29, No. 4, pp. 297–318.

Parsons Talcott, 2009, *System społeczny*, Kraków: NOMOS.

Pauluk Dorota, 2016, *Ukryte programy uniwersyteckiej edukacji ich rezultaty*, Kraków: UJ.

Peach Robert L., Yaliraki Sophia N., LeFevre David, Barahona Mauricio, 2020, 'Data-Driven Unsupervised Clustering of Online Learner behaviour', Science of Learning, Vol. 4, pp. 1–11.

Pensiero Nicola, Kelly Anthony, Bokhove Christian, 2020, 'Learning Inequalities during the Covid-19 Pandemic: How Families Cope with Home-Schooling', University of Southampton, (Retrieved from: https://eprints.soton.ac.uk/442619/).

Plebańska Marlena, Szyller Aleksandra, Sieńczewska Małgorzata, 2020, Raport Librus, 'Edukacja Zdalna w czasach Covid-19', UW, (Retrieved from: https://kometa.edu.pl/uploads/publication/941/24a2_A_a_nauczanie_zdalne_oczami_nauczycieli_i_uczniow_RAPORT.pdf?v2.8).

Ptaszek Grzegorz., Bigaj Magdalena, Dębski Maciej, Pyżalski Jacek, Stunża Grzegorz, 2020, 'Zdalne nauczanie a adaptacja do warunków społecznych w czasie epidemii koronawirusa', Warszawa (Retrieved from: https://www.cen.gda.pl/download/2020-09/4024.pdf_).

Rayman M. Paula, 2014, *Kibbutz Community and Nation Building*, Princeton Legacy Library.
Riesmann David, 1996, *Samotny tłum*, Warszawa: MUZA S.A.
Reay Diane, 2017, *Miseducation: Inequality, Education and the Working Classes*, Policy Press.
Reay Diane, 2020, 'English Education in the Time of Coronavirus', FORUM, Vol. 62, No. 3, pp. 311–323.
Reid Ivan, 1978, *Sociological Perspectives on School and Education*, London: Open Books.
Renton Alex, 2017, *Stiff Upper Lip*, Orion, Great Britain
'Research and analysis GCSE, AS and A level', Summer Report, 2021, (Retrieved from: https://www.gov.uk/government/publications/gcse-as-and-a-level-summer-report-2021_).
Research Report, 2021, 'Digital Divide in UK Education during COVID-19 Pandemic: Literature Review', Cambridge Assessment.
Romaniuk Miłosz Wawrzyniec, Łukasiewicz-Wieleba Joanna, 2022, 'Hybrid Education in Higher Education on the Example of Students Experiences in Post-Pandemic Reality', International Journal of Electronics and Telecommunications, Vol. 68, No. 3, pp. 497–504 (Retrieved from: https://journals.pan.pl/dlibra/show-content?id=124258).
Rosenthal Robert, Jacobson Lenore, 1969, Pygmalion in the Classroom, The Urban Review, Vol. 240, pp. 16–20.
Rovai, Alfred, 2002, Sense of community, perceived cognitive learning, and persistence in asynchronous learning networks, The Internet and Higher Education, Vol. 5, Issue 4, pp. 319–332
'RS Assessment', 2021, (Retrieved from: https://www.risingstars-uk.com/media/Rising-Stars/Catalogue/RS-assessment-cat-and-order-form-2021-web.pdf).
Sa Maria Jose, Serpa Sandro, 2020, 'COVID-19 and the Promotion of Digital Competences in Education', Universal Journal of Educational Research, Vol. 8, No. 10, pp. 4520–4528.
Sadura Przemyslaw, 2017, *Państwo, szkola, klasy*, Warszawa: Wydawnictwo Krytyki Politycznej.
Scambler Graham, 2020, 'A Sociological Autobiography: 94 – The Fractured Society', (Retrieved from: http://www.grahamscambler.com/a-sociological-autobiography-94-the-fractured-society/).
Schaub Maryellen, 2010, 'Parenting Cognitive Development: The Institutional Effects of Mass Education on the Social Construction of Childhood and Parenting', Sociology of Education, Vol. 83, No. 1, pp. 46–66.
Sekścińska Katarzyna, Trzcińska Agata, Gurba Krzysztof, Lackowski Jerzy, Cieślik Łukasz, Dynowska-Chmielewska Krystyna, Długosz Piotr, Dankiewicz-Berger Malwina, Muchacki Mateusz, 2020, 'Raport z badania, 2020, Kształcenie na odległość oczami dyrektorów szkół, nauczycieli, uczniów i rodziców', Centrum Polityk Publicznych, (Retrieved from: https://politykipubliczne.pl/wp-content/uploads/2020/10/11-Raport-oczami-dyrketorow_Sekscinska23.09.2020-last.pdf).

Seul Sylwia, 1991, Wpływ oczekiwań nauczyciela na zachowanie i osiągnięcia uczniów, NEODIDAGMATA XX, pp. 53–63.

Seul Sylwia, 1995, *Oczekiwania nauczyciela a wyniki nauczania*, Szczecin: US.

Sharp Caroline, Nelson Julie, Lucas Megan, Julius Jenna, McCrone Tami, Sims David, 2020, Schools' responses to COVID-19. The challenges facing schools and pupils in September 2020. Published by the National Foundation for Educational Research. Slough: NFER.

Sorokin Pitrim A. 2009, *Ruchliwość społeczna*, tłum. Jerzyna Słomczyńska, Warszawa: Wydawnictwo Instytutu Filozofii i Socjologii PAN.

Spiecker Ben, 1984, 'The Pedagogical Relationship', Oxford Review of Education, Vol. 10, No. 2, pp. 203–210.

Sterna Dorota, 2020, 'Ocenianie w dobie Koronawirusa' [in:] Pyżalski red. *Edukacja w czasie pandemii wirusa COVID-19. Z dystansem o tym, co robimy jako nauczyciele.*, edukacja, (Retrieved from: https://www.edu-akcja.pl/wydawnictwa/zdalnie/).

Stunża Grzegorz, 2020, Zdania (nie)dokoczone. Edukacja zdalna w wypowiedziach uczniów, rodziców i nauczycieli. Jakościowy moduł badawczy w: Ptaszek Grzegorz (ed.), *'Edukacja zdalna: co się stało z uczniami, ich rodzicami i nauczycielami?'*, Gdańskie: Gdańskie Wydawnictwo Psychologiczne.

Szacka Barbara, 2003, *Wprowadzenie do socjologii*, Warszawa: Oficyna Naukowa.

Ślusarczyk Magdalena, Świątkiewicz-Mośny Maria, 2020, Disappearing children – How the COVID-19 pandemic reinforces inequalities and social problems in Poland in: Lombardi Lia (ed.), *The Challenges of Covid-19: Global Health and Inequality*, Newsletter 11, Vol. 16, pp. 33–35.

Tarabini Aina, 2021, 'The Role of Schooling in Times of Global Pandemic: A Sociological Approach', International Studies in Sociology of Education, Vol. 31, No. 4, pp. 1–19.

Teacher Tapp, 2020, 'Monitoring COVID-19 Readiness in Schools', (Retrieved from: https://teachertapp.co.uk/monitoring-covid-19-readiness-in-schools/).

'Timeline of UK Coronavirus Lockdowns, March 2020 to March 2021', Institute for Government Analysis, (Retrieved from: https://www.institute-forgovernment.org.uk/sites/default/files/timeline-lockdown-web.pdf).

Toffler Alvin, 1986, *Trzecia fala*, tłum. Ewa Woydyłło, Warszawa: PIW.

Turner Ralph, 1971, Sponsored and contest mobility and the school system in: Earl Hopper (eds.), *Readings in the Theory of Educational System*, London: Hutchinson, pp. 71–90.

Turner Victor, 2005, *Gry społeczne, pola i metafory. Symboliczne działanie w społeczeństwie*, tłum. Wojciech Usakiewicz, Kraków: Wydawnictwo Uniwersytetu Jagiellońskiego.

Tzuo Pei Wen 1, Yang Chien Hui 1, Wright Susan Kay, 2021, 'Child-Centered Education: Incorporating Reconceptualism and Poststructuralism', Educational Research and Reviews, Vol. 6, No. 8, pp. 554–559.

UNESCO, 2020, Global Education Coalition, Message from Audrey Azoulay, UNESCO Director-General, (Retrieved from: https://en.unesco.org/covid19/educationresponse/globalcoalition).

UNICEF, 2020, 'Children in Lockdown: Rapid Assessment of the Impact of Coronavirus on Children in the UK', (Retrieved from: https://www.unicef.org.uk/wp-content/uploads/2020/04/UnicefUK_ChildrenInLockdown_RapidAssessment.pdf).

United Nations, 2020, 'Policy Brief: Education during COVID-19 and beyond', (Retrieved from: https://www.un.org/development/desa/dspd/wpcontent/uploads/sites/22/2020/08/sg_policy_brief_covid-19_and_education_august_2020.pdf).

United Nations, 2021, 'The Sustainable Development Goals Report', (Retrieved in: https://www.un.org/sustainabledevelopment/progress-report/).

Ward Randolph E., Burke Mary Ann, 2004, *Improving Achievement in Low-Performing Schools. Key Results for School Leaders*, California: Sage.

Willis Paul E., 1977, *Learning to Labor: How Working-Class Kids Get Working Class Jobs*, Lexington: Lexington Books.

Woods Peter, 1983, *Sociology and the School: An Interactionist Viewpoint*, London: Routledge and Kegan Paul.

Woods Peter, 1986, *Inside Schools. Ethnography in Educational Research*, London: Routledge and Kegan Paul.

World Economic Forum, 2022, (Retrieved from: https://www.weforum.org/agenda/2022/05/can-technology-save-the-world/).

Woźniak Olga, 2019, 'Skończmy już z tymi testami! Celem szkoły jest rozwój a nie uczenie się pod testy', in: Gazeta Wyborcza, (Retrieved from: https://wyborcza.pl/7,75400,24816343,skonczmy-juz-z-tymi-z-testami.html).

Young Michael, (ed.), 1971, *Knowledge and Control: New Directions for the Sociology of Education*, London: Collier-Macmillan.

Zemło Mariusz, 1996, *Nowa socjologia edukacji*, Białystok: Trans-Humana.

Zhao Yong, 2020, 'Tofu Is Not Cheese: Rethinking Education Amid the COVID-19 Pandemic', ECNU Review of Education, Vol. 3, No. 2, pp. 189–203.

Zhao Yong, 2020, 'COVID-19 as a Catalyst for Educational Change', Prospects, Vol. 49, pp. 29–33.

Zhao Yong, Watterston Jim, 2021, 'The Changes We Need: Education Post COVID-19', Journal of Educational Change, Vol. 22, pp. 3–12.

Znaniecki Florian, 2001, *Socjologia wychowania*, Warszawa: PWN.

Index

Note: Page numbers containing tables are shown in **bold**, and figures are shown in *italic*, respectively, in the following.

allocation, 3, 30, 32, 36, 40, 44, 47, **49**, 50, 52, 54–55, *56*, 59, 65, 67, 71, 73–74, 77–78, 81, 85–86, 88, 90
allocative approach, 46, 52
allocative dimension, *57*
allocative function, 54
ascriptive approach, 47, 48
asynchronous mode, 7

blended learning, 8, 92
bureaucratisation, 34

comprehensive schooling model, 3
conflict approach, 46, **49**, 53
contest mobility, 66, 103
credentialism, 48, 67

democratic society, 40, 41
digital divide, 1, 17–18, 21–23, 88
digitisation, 1, 2
distance education, 1, 3, 5–6, 12, 17, 19–20, 27, 29, 77, 79–80, 83, 88, 92
distance learning, 1, 2, 11–14, 17–18, 20, 22–23, 25, 27, 28–29, 80, 92
division of labour, 35, 85

education, 1–48, **49**, 50–52, 54–56, 59, 63–64, 66–68, 71–97, 99–100
education system, 2–4, 8–10, 24, 27, 29–33, 35–36, 52, 55–56, 59, 66–67, 72, 74, 77, 80, 82, 85–88, 91–93
educational change, 5, 19, 27, 82, 92

educational crisis, 2, 28
educational disruption, 5, 28
educational expansion, 32
educational inequalities, 1, 6, 9, 87
educationalisation, 32
emerging society, 37

face-to-face (F2F) learning, 8
functional approach, 45–46, **49**, 50, 54
functional stratification theory, 48

habitus, 59, 68
hidden curriculum, 30, 69–70, 79, 82
human capital theory, 48
hybrid learning, 7, 12

individualisation, 34
industrialisation, 31, 34–35
institutional dimension, *57*
institutionalisation, 3, 30, 61
interpretative approach, 46, **49**, 54

learning losses, 6, 22, 24

mass education, 3, 33, 35–36, 38–39, 42, 86, 93
mass schooling. *See* mass education
meritocracy, 36, 66, 77, 87
modern rationalisation, 33
modern societies, 3, 4, 31–32, 43, 55, 71, 81, 90–93

modernisation, 31, 33, 38, 42, 47, 86
modernity, 31, 33, 72, 89–90

neo-institutionalism, 48
neo-Marxism, 47–48

online education. *See* distance learning
ontological security, 2

pedagogical relation, 7, 71–72, 77
pedagogical relationship, 30, 58, 59, 64–68, 72–75, 77–78, 81–86, 88–89, 91, 93
post-industrial society, 33

rationalisation, 34, 98
reflexive modernisation. *See* modernisation
regionalisation, 7, 61, 64–65, 71, 74, 82, 85
remote learning. *See* distance learning
ritual. *See* rituals
ritualisation, 63
rituals, 2, 7, 29, 53, 60–64, 67, 69, 71–72, 75–77, 85–86
routinisation, 7, 61, 64–65, 67, 71, 91

school, 1–15, 18–23, 25, 27–33, 35–36, 40, 43–47, 50–55, 56, 57–93, 103
school culture, 1–3, 8, 28–29, 33, 55, 59, 67, 71, 73, 80, 90, 92
schooled society, 3, 30–32, 94
schooling, 1–7, 9–10, 17, 23, 25, 29–33, 40, 44, 46, 50, 55–56, 57, 58–59, 69, 71–73, 78, 80–82, 85, 87, 89, 90–92, 101
social class, 1, 6, 9–10
social mobility, 33, 41, 73, 88
social structure, 35–36, 40, 46, 48–50, 60–61, 86, 90
socialisation, 3, 29–30, 32, 35–38, 43–44, 46–47, **49**, 50–55, 56, 65, 68–71, 73–74, 78–79, 81, 85–86, 90, 93
socialisation dimension, 57
structural functionalism, 47, 51
synchronous mode, 7
systemic needs, 31, 71, 81, 91

technological innovation, 35

urbanisation, 34

For Product Safety Concerns and Information please contact our EU representative GPSR@taylorandfrancis.com
Taylor & Francis Verlag GmbH, Kaufingerstraße 24, 80331 München, Germany

www.ingramcontent.com/pod-product-compliance
Lightning Source LLC
Chambersburg PA
CBHW051756230426
43670CB00012B/2318